INTERNATIONAL
MOTOR
RACING

ERNATIONAL MOTOR RACING

DOUG NYE

Contents The motor racing story/10 Racing and race spectating/42 The racing car/62 The men/71 The circuits/83 Winners' tables/89 Index and further reading/92

LEISUREGUIDES/MACMILLAN

Front endpapers. Indianapolis 1972. A
'rolling' start—the grid is given the green
flag. Frontispiece: The pits during practice.
Title pages: Jacky Ickx leads the field at
Clermont. Opposite: Ray Harroun, winner of
the first Indianapolis 500, 1911

Acknowledgements

All photographs in this book were taken by
Geoffrey Goddard with the exception of the
following:

Barnaby's 24; Peter Coltrin 68; Conway Picture
Library 24m, b; Indianapolis Motor Speedway
8–9, 41n, 47t, 80L, front and back endpapers;
London Art Tech 76R; George Monkhouse 14t,
b, 25t; Doug Nye 49t, b colour; 66–9b;
C. Posthumus 21t, b; RTHPL 13, 14, 21m, 26;
Renault Ltd 10–11, 15; Syndication International
6, 46

SBN 333 148 762

Design by Paul Watkins

Illustration Research by Susan Mayhew

Drawings by Richard Osborne
and Suzanne Stevenson

First published 1973 by
Macmillan London Limited
London and Basingstoke
Associated companies in New York,
Toronto, Dublin, Melbourne,
Johannesburg and Madras

Phototypeset by Oliver Burridge Filmsetting Limited,
Crawley, Sussex
Printed in Japan by Dai Nippon Printing Company

INTRODUCTION

Motor racing is one of the most exciting, most spectacular, and most misunderstood of modern sports. It has a long history, and its purest forms of Grand Prix and Indianapolis-type track racing may be traced virtually unbroken, from 1906 and 1911 respectively, to the present day. Today there is more motor racing in more classes and in more parts of the world than ever before, and more people are going along to watch it.

This guide to the sport fills in the historical background to what goes on out there on the circuits of the world, and it explains what motor racing is all about, how the subtleties of driving technique and car design operate, and examines the personalities behind today's headlines. There is much more to the sport than immediately meets the eye, and anybody who thinks that racing drivers are simply young maniacs forcing their cars along as fast as they can possibly go is wildly mistaken. Top-class race driving is an art which demands extraordinary perception, reflex and coordination from men who are as much athletes as are top-class tennis players, fencers or footballers.

It is a team-game until the flag falls for the start of the motor race, whereupon the mechanics who built and prepared the car must stand back and it is all down to the lonely figure in the cockpit to make their baby operate.

We hope this guide will give insight into this majestic sport and into the lonely skills of the men who have become its greats.

1 THE MOTOR RACING STORY

Carl Benz produced the world's first practical motor car in Mannheim, Germany in 1885. In the years which followed, motoring gained a tightening grip on the aristocracy, the *nouveau riche* and the tradesmen of a rapidly industrializing world.

It was inevitable that someone, somewhere, should sometime claim that his Benz was quicker than his friend's Panhard-Levassor or Daimler. So the first private, unpublicized and unrecorded motoring competitions must have come about.

Then, after only nine years of the horseless carriage, what is acknowledged as the first-ever properly organized motor sporting event took place in France. It was a reliability run from Paris to Rouen, organized by the Paris paper *Le Petit Journal*, for a prize of £200.

The course ran for $74\frac{1}{2}$ miles along the valley of the Seine, and Georges Bouton arrived first in his own De Dion-Bouton steam tractor, which towed a normally horse-drawn carriage from which the front wheels had been removed. His drive lasted 4 hours and 40 minutes, averaging around 12mph, but the organizers didn't accept his vehicle as an automobile as defined in their regulations, and so his performance was ruled out and the prize divided between the Peugeot brothers' cars and Emil Levassor's Panhard.

Early motor racing; the Renault light car team lined up before the Paris–Bordeaux race of 1901. Left to right: Louis Renault, his brother Marcel, Dury and Grus

This trial was a great success, and in November of 1894 the first-ever motoring competition committee was formed and planned the first true road race for the following summer.

The plan was for a round trip, city-to-city, and there was nothing small minded about the course chosen. The two cities in question were to be Paris and the port of Bordeaux on the Atlantic coast, and the race distance was no less than 732 miles!

The organizers countered charges of recklessness by saying that of necessity reliability must go hand in hand with speed in an event as long as this, and in fact they discouraged the fastest types of car then built by stipulating that two-seater cars would not be eligible for first prize. Entries and donations to the prize fund poured in, until 45 vehicles were ready to fight it out for a staggering total fund of £2,800.

At nine o'clock on the morning of 11 June 1895, the field got away from the start in the *Place de l'Etoile* and processed to Versailles, whence the race proper began on open roads. Only 22 survivors left Versailles, and after 48 hours and 48 minutes without rest, sleep or a stop for food, Emil Levassor came clattering back to the Porte Maillot aboard a wheezing and travel stained Panhard-Levassor.

His staggering performance, in which he refused to hand over to his relief drivers for fear of their losing his hard-won lead, is recorded as the first-ever major race win, but in fact the car was a two-seater, and so he was robbed of the first prize—this going to Koechlin's Peugeot, which was third on the road, taking over 59 hours for the 732 miles. Levassor was classified second and Rigoulot third in the second-on-the-road Peugeot.

This event was such a wonderful success that its organizing Committee formed the *Automobile Club de France* at the end of the year.

By 1897 the great age of city-to-city races was under way, but the sport had already claimed its first victims, including Levassor who swerved to avoid a dog in the 1896 Paris–Marseilles–Paris and crashed into a ditch, dying from his injuries a year later.

Panhards were the most successful competitors at the time, and today the scene can only be imagined as these rickety early motor vehicles clattered, smoked and steamed their way along the dusty, tree and ditch-lined roads of France; watched by peasants clustered in the doors of their cottages, open-mouthed with that exciting mixture of fear and wonderment.

The first capital-to-capital race took place in 1898, over a course of 895 miles to be tackled in stages between Paris and Amsterdam. Fernand Charron won in a Panhard, a mark of progress being its rated output of 8hp and its winning average speed of 29mph!

This was fast, showing a much higher maximum speed than the first World's Land Speed Record which was set-up that year at a special *course de vitesse*, in Acheres Park, near St Germain to the north of Paris. The Comte de Chasseloup-Laubat set the first record at 39.245mph in his Jeantaud electric car, but just to put the record in perspective the meeting's fastest cyclist beat the good Count's flying kilometre time by a clear second!

The heroic age
Through the closing years of the nineteenth century the great city-to-city marathons swept on, and the first twelve months of our century saw the first race to be run on a closed circuit; the *Circuit du Sud-Ouest* around the old city of Pau in Southern France. The 208-mile race fell to De Knyff's 16hp 4.4-litre Panhard, at the speed of 43.5mph.

In June, 1900 the first of a new series of races was held for the Gordon Bennett Trophy, which was donated by the same American newspaper magnate who had sponsored H. M. Stanley's success-ful quest for Dr Livingstone through the African bush. Bennett's competition was for teams of three cars from each motor manu-facturing country; the teams to be nominated by their national clubs. The winner of the trophy would have to organize the follow-ing year's event, and so a truly International competition was established for the first time.

Louis Renault arriving at Bordeaux in the tragic Paris Madrid race of 1903, is told of his brother Marcel's fatal accident

This grand scheme was to become the progenitor of Grand Prix racing, and it instituted racing to an agreed International set of regulations, or 'Formula'. Unfortunately the race was to become largely a French preserve, falling to the only two finishers (both Panhards driven by Charron and Girardot) in the first 351-mile race from Paris–Lyons! In 1901 interest in the Trophy was so limited that it was run as a mere class within the Paris–Bordeaux race; Girardot's Panhard keeping the Trophy in France.

It looked as though the competition was about to die lying down when in 1902 the English won the Trophy. . . . The French organizers awarded it for the Paris–Innsbruck section of an exceptionally gruelling race to Vienna, and Selwyn Francis Edge took the honours with the only survivor; his 45hp 6.4-litre Napier!

So the Trophy survived, with the 1903 event run on an Irish course around the Curragh. British law made the closing of public roads for races impossible, unlike most of the countries of Europe, and so the RAC had to promote their events in Ireland or on the Isle of Man. The Trophy should have represented the main stream of racing development, but in practice it was overshadowed by the great inter-city blinds, until the tragic 24th of May, 1903.

That was the first day of the Paris–Madrid race, which started from the usual line at Versailles. Speeds were tremendous; too tremendous for many of the cars which failed to reach the first control at Rambouillet. Louis Renault took the lead with his light 30hp car, and it is said that he covered a section between Bonneval and Chartres at an average of nearly *ninety* miles per hour. But behind him his brother Marcel lost control of his Renault while moving up through the field, tumbled in a ditch and was killed.

Above: Baron Pierre de Crawhez, winner of the Circuit des Ardennes race in 1903. Circuit races were to replace inter-city events after this year. Right: Ferenc Szisz and the 1906 Renault, winner of the first ever Grand Prix

Lorraine Barrow avoided a dog only to hit a tree, killing riding mechanic Pierre Rodez instantly and himself dying from his injuries within a few hours. Stead was fearfully hurt in another crash, and Leslie Porter crashed trying to avoid a closed level crossing gate—killing his mechanic, Nixon. Tourand's mechanic died when their car ploughed into the crowd outside Angouleme, crushing two spectators, and so the disaster mushroomed. Soon the telegraph was buzzing between Bordeaux and the capital, and the authorities immediately ordered the race to be abandoned, and all competing cars to be rail-freighted back to Paris.

So the great age of inter-city racing ground to an abrupt halt, while racing on lengthy closed public road courses, such as the Circuit des Ardennes became standard. The British Bennett round was the most successful so far, with teams from Germany, France and the USA facing the home trio.

Camille Jenatzy, the red-bearded Belgian, took the Trophy for Germany at the wheel of a 60hp 9.2-litre Mercedes, and then in 1904 Leon Thery's 80hp 10-litre Richard-Brasier retook the Trophy for France, in front of the Kaiser on German soil. In 1905 the last Gordon Bennett race was run over 341 miles in the Auvergne, and Thery won again, this time with an 11-litre Richard-Brasier.

The French held that it was unfair to limit an industry as large and diverse as their's to just three entries, and they gave notice that they would not be running another Gordon Bennett race in 1906—they would be replacing it with their own 'Grand Prix' which would be open virtually to all comers.

Motor racing had taken on such an International aspect by this time that it required an Internationally-recognized governing body, both for the sport in particular and for automobile affairs in general. Thus the 'International Association of Recognized Automobile Clubs', or AIACR.

America was almost as lively a racing scene as France, and

this pre-Grand Prix age had seen the Vanderbilt Cup races instituted on Long Island by millionaire W. K. Vanderbilt, thus bringing the might of early circuit racing across the Atlantic. Long Island races were marred by a dreadful lack of spectator control, and there were some really nasty accidents. But even there the French industry ruled supreme, George Heath's Panhard winning the inaugural event in 1904 and Victor Hemery's Darracq the second in 1905.

The first Grand Prix
Then 1906 saw the dawn of the Grand Prix age, with the autocratic French club organizing the first of their 'Great Prize' races over a 65-mile mixed public and artificial road course near Le Mans. The race was to be held on two days, six laps on each day totalling 767 miles.

The entry was hardly representative of the world's new motor industry, but Renault won the day with their bright red 90hp 12.8-litre machine driven by Ferenc Szisz. He was a 33-year-old Hungarian, formerly Louis Renault's riding mechanic, his apparently unpronounceable surname being uttered 'Zizz' or 'Chitch' dependent upon to whom you are talking! He completed the stages in 12 hours 14 minutes and 7 seconds, averaging a very impressive 63.0mph to become history's first Grand Prix winner.

So Grand Prix racing was born, and in its wake manufacturers began building specialized racing machines, bearing little relation to everyday road-going models. Two seater bodies were retained to accommodate the riding mechanic and driver, but they were stark in the extreme, leaving the intrepid crew exposed.

Engines were commonly of four cylinders, each of 3–4-litres *per cylinder*, steel chassis frames were replacing armoured wood, and honeycomb radiators were replacing the gilled-tube types.

In the years that followed, the Grand Prix was run until 1909

The parade of motor cars at the
opening of H. F. Locke King's
Brooklands motor course in June, 1907.
Here the cavalcade is just joining the
Member's Banking after negotiating the
start-to-finish straight

when a trading depression hit the European factories, and they
agreed not to contest Grand Prix racing—for the cars used had
by this time become rather unedifying luxuries, so far removed
were they from production practise. The French Grand Prix was
abandoned for lack of entries, and it was not to be revived until
1911, when a poorly-supported race at Le Mans was dubbed 'The
Old Crocks Grand Prix'. In 1912 the ACF decided to abandon all
the restrictive legislation which had grown up over the years, and
they threw their Grand Prix open to virtually all comers. This had
an interesting effect, for while Grand Prix racing had been shelved
the interested manufacturers had still been gaining publicity by
contesting 'Voiturette' events for small-capacity production-type
light cars.

The Grand Prix of 1912 at Dieppe saw giant cars of the old order
facing the new 'Voiturettes' and some in-between sized cars from
the successful new manufacturers such as Peugeot and Sunbeam, and the result found a French winner in Georges Boillot's
'medium' 7.6-litre Peugeot, from Louis Wagner's monster 15-litre
Fiat and Victor Rigal's 3-litre Sunbeam 'Voiturette'.

While GP cars had borne little relation to the production cars
of the time (a cry which we hear so often today, and which many
people seem to think is a *new* state of affairs) top-class racing
such as this still acted as a forcing house for ideas. In this it was
not alone, and when H. F. Locke-King opened his 2½-mile banked
Brooklands test and race circuit in England in 1907 he fired British
designers' imagination in a completely new direction. Very high
speeds were attainable on Brooklands' scientifically-designed

speed bowl, the bankings being angled so that at given speeds a car would ride round them without any deflection of the steering. Aerodynamics became uppermost in some designers' minds, and the enclosed cockpit sides, slim profiles and long tapering tails bred at Brooklands track-racing experience quickly found their way into GP racing.

Indianapolis is born
Across the Atlantic the first United States Grand Prix race had been run at Savannah in 1908, again being dominated by European cars, and in 1909 Carl Fisher and some business associates opened their $2\frac{1}{2}$-mile Indianapolis Motor Speedway—modelled along Brooklands lines.

The first Indy race, a two-lap sprint, fell to Louis Schwitzer's Stoddard-Dayton at 57mph, and two years later the first of the classic line of 500-mile races was held there, with Ray Harroun winning in a 6-cylinder Marmon at 74.4mph. Racing in America began to develop its own unique character with the opening of Indianapolis and of the banked wooden board track at Playa del Rey, California, in 1910. This compact, 1-mile track, made an exciting spectacle for paying spectators, who could themselves be better marshalled (and made to pay for the privilege) than could those on the vast open-road courses of Europe.

So while Europe went the road racing way, and Brooklands developed its own specialized breed of track racers, American motor racing began to concentrate on what the public wanted—and that was thrills and spills galore on a circuit short enough for everybody to see *all* the action. The board tracks were particularly popular, being cheap to construct and offering exciting racing, and in later years they bred their own kinds of cars—the first pure single-seater racers.

Back in Europe Boillot scored his second consecutive Grand Prix victory for Peugeot in 1913, and in 1914 looked all set for his hat-trick in what has become one of the greatest Grand Prix races of all time, held on the Givors Circuit, near Lyons.

Teams were entered by no less than fourteen major manufacturers, and Boillot fought a gallant battle with the regimentally directed Mercedes team until his car broke down just 12 miles from the finish. German Mercedes came home first, second and third, with the 1908 winner Christian Lautenschlager winning for the second time, and leading team-mates Wagner and Sailer. So the legend of Mercedes domination in Grand Prix racing was born, but just a month after the race at Lyons France and Germany met in a much grimmer contest—the First World War.

While Europe tore itself apart, racing continued in America, with the Indianapolis 500-Miles of 1915 and 1916 falling to Ralph de Palma's Grand Prix type Mercedes and Dario Resta's Peugeot respectively. The last year of peace had seen the complete changing of the racing order in Europe, with the old 15–18-litre monsters ousted by the new lightweight $4\frac{1}{2}$-litre cars with multi-cylinder engines. Mors, Panhard, Renault, Richard-Brasier were names missing from the entry lists; replaced by the new 'Voiturette' based companies of Peugeot, Mercedes, Schneider, Delage, Sunbeam and Vauxhall.

When peace settled in 1918 the return to normality was a painfully slow process, but in 1919 the Indianapolis classic was revived with Howdy Wilcox winning in a Peugeot, and in Sicily the ancient Targa Florio was run again, producing another Peugeot win for Andre Boillot—younger brother of the extrovert pre-war Champion, who had been killed flying.

In 1920 the first post-war Grand Prix Formula was fixed by the AIACR, limiting engine size to 3-litres, with a minimum weight of $14\frac{1}{2}$cwt. But racing was restricted to America until 1921, when the revived French Grand Prix took place over a desperately ill-surfaced Le Mans circuit. Fred and Augie Duesenberg, whose cars had been having much success in America, shipped over a team for the Grand Prix, and their star driver Jimmy Murphy actually won, beating the French Ballots team.

This Grand Prix was notable for several reasons. Firstly it marked America's first—and last until 1967—triumph over European GP machinery. Then, back in 1908 trenches had been dug at the side of the Dieppe circuit to act as service, refuelling and tyre change depots for the competing cars, and thus the word 'pit' came to have its motor racing meaning. The '21 Grand Prix saw the trench-type pit abandoned in favour of a road-level structure, as used today although the name 'pit' has survived.

The Duesenbergs used hydraulically operated brakes for the first time, and Ballot and Fiat both used mechanical brake servos. The year also saw the prophetic first use of supercharging in European racing, when Mercedes used the system in the Coppa Florio.

'Supercharging' means using a mechanical system to force petrol-air mixture under pressure into the engine cylinders, instead of relying upon natural atmospheric pressure to do the job. The more you could ram in, the more power you could find in return, and the supercharger was soon to become an indispensable part of the racing scene. Chadwick in America had first used supercharging in 1907, so this was another example of American innovation being developed in Europe, instead of vice versa as in so many other things.

In 1922 a 2-litre capacity limit was slapped on GP racing, and the Italians built the first artificial road circuit through the Royal Park at Monza, just north of Milan, and the new Autodrome there saw the first national Grand Prix to join the French event. Pietro Bordino won it at the wheel of a Fiat, while his team-mate Felice Nazzaro won the French classic at Strasbourg.

Sunbeam and Alfa Romeo came to challenge Fiat's supremacy in the 2-litre Formula races of 1923–24, as their designers tended to reproduce the successful Fiat designs of 1922! The '23 season saw Delage introducing the V12-cylinder engine to road racing; Voisin and Bugatti introduced all-enveloping streamlined bodies; Fiat scored the first Grand Prix success for a supercharged engine in the European GP at Monza; and Benz turned out the first rear-engined GP car in the same event. . . .

In 1924 all Grand Prix events (now including those at San Sebastian in Spain and Monza in Italy in addition to the French race at Lyons) were won by supercharged cars. Sir Henry Segrave won for Sunbeam in Spain, while Alfa Romeo won the other two events with Campari in France and Ascari at Monza.

Segrave's GP win was to be the last for an English driver in an English car until 1955, but the race was marred by an accident to team-mate Kenelm Lee Guinness's Sunbeam, in which the riding mechanic was killed. This triggered a new ruling for 1925, in which riding mechanics were banned.

France's Montlhery Autodrome, just south of Paris, saw the ACF Grand Prix for the first time on an artificial course, and this was the first such race to be run on a Sunday, as is now the custom world-wide save for dear old England. The race was tragically marred by Ascari's fatal accident in an Alfa Romeo, while leading, and after the Italian team's withdrawal the Delage shared by Robert Benoist and Albert Divo scored a home win. Ascari had just won the first Belgian GP on a new circuit at Spa-Francorchamps, and his loss was a bitter one for Alfa Romeo.

Then came a change of Formula in 1926, when engine capacity was slashed to only 1500cc to combat ever-increasing speeds, and a minimum weight limit for the cars was set at $11\frac{3}{4}$cwt. In 1927 the Formula continued, although the mechanic's unoccupied seat need no longer be carried. This was the age of Bugatti and Delage, the former using two-seater road/race cars and the latter more specialized offset single-seaters, with a right-hand driving position and two-seater body width to suit the Formula.

Once again Grand Prix racing proved prohibitively expensive, and when the major specialist manufacturers such as Delage and Talbot pulled out the Formula was shelved and race promoters began to run their events for almost anything going. Entries came from individuals operating as amateurs just for the sport or as professionals for gain, and many of the 2-litre cars of the 1922–25 Formula were revived for racing. Two-seater cars ran in Grand Prix races with their road-going wings and lights removed, while with them in place they competed as sports cars in events such as the Le Mans 24-Hours, and the RAC Tourist Trophy.

During 1929 and 1930 Alfa Romeo, Bugatti and Maserati—the new Italian manufacturer—dominated the results lists, with drivers such as Louis Chiron, Achille Varzi, and Tazio Nuvolari.

America breeds the single-seater

In America the track-racing scene had developed with Miller and Duesenberg cars dominant, using twin overhead camshaft engines owing much to the fine old Peugeots of the First World War period in slender purely single-seater chassis. Both marques sent representatives across the Atlantic to the 1927 Italian GP, this event marking the European road racing debut of pure single central-seater racing cars.

From 1930–33 there was no restriction placed on the size of either engine or car in Grand Prix racing, and a great number of experiments were made with engines of between four and five litres capacity, developing around 300hp, but they were unsuccessful. These years of free-for-all racing saw the reintroduction of pure racing designs, owing little to road practice and incapable of schizophrenic adjustment from GP to sports car guise. Alfa Romeo, Bugatti and Maserati continued their dominance of the racing scene and in 1932 the former company introduced their immortal P3 'Monoposto' design—the first successful true single-seater in European road-racing. The cars won everything in sight, and in 1933 Maserati turned out a super-slim single-seater to combat them, reintroducing hydraulic brake systems years after Duesenberg's striking success at Le Mans.

Formule Libre racing saw some really fearsome cars produced, such as a 16-cylinder by Maserati, and later twin-engined cars by Alfa Romeo in which the intrepid driver sat in his cockpit, sandwiched by one engine ahead, and another in behind. . . .

Then in 1934 a new Formula was introduced, replacing the years of Formule Libre which had seen top-class road racing regaining much of its former glory. Regulations dictated a *maximum* weight of 750Kg, with free engine size and a minimum car body width. The years of Italian domination of racing with the Alfa Romeo and Maserati cars had had their effect upon the propaganda chiefs of the new Nazi state in Germany, and the new regulations attracted state-supported participation from Mercedes-Benz and the new Auto Union combine. Both firms produced striking new designs, featuring all-independent suspension, streamlined bodies and powerful engines, and Auto Union mounted their 16-cylinder engine *behind* the driver's cockpit.

Alfa Romeo, Maserati and Bugatti all updated their cars to comply with the new regulations, although the French marque's bolt was nearly shot, and during the life of the 750Kg Formula the silver cars from Germany were completely dominant.

The Italian cars of the old era had used engines whose output far exceeded the road-holding abilities of their chassis, and the German designers produced rigid chassis with soft all-independent suspension, allowing the cars' road wheels to follow the road surface fairly faithfully and so make full use of both engine power and braking.

23

Between 1934 and 1937 Auto Union won 18 major races, Mercedes-Benz won 22 and these totals left only eight other laurels to be taken, most of them falling to the irrepressible Nuvolari's Alfa Romeos. The swarthy little Italian Champion became a legend in his own lifetime, and he was completely idolized in his own country before the age of German domination began. As it progressed, and as he took on nine German cars and beat them all in the German GP of 1935, he was almost deified. But even his skills and spirit were not enough to keep outdated machinery competitive, and in 1938 he joined the Auto Union team, replacing their ex-motor-cycle star Bernd Rosemeyer who had been killed in a record attempt on a German Autobahn.

The great names of the 750Kg Formula were Hans Stuck—the lofty Austrian who drove for Auto Union—Rudolf Caracciola, the greatest of all Mercedes drivers, who shone in wet weather races —and then there was Dick Seaman, a rising English driver who joined the Mercedes team in 1937 after a splendid 1936 season racing and winning in a rebuilt but still ten years old ex-GP Delage.

This car had been contesting the 1500cc Voiturette class, which had been dominated by ERA and Maserati since 1934. Seaman had it modified and updated, and his single-minded approach to a professional race driving career made him Britain's first such driver to achieve International stature.

Left: Caracciola with the difficult 1936 Mercedes-Benz in the Hungarian GP at Budapest. Below: Dick Seaman in the 1938 Mercedes during the Swiss GP at Berne

Left: The great Nuvolari takes the trophy at Donington, 1938. Below: Nuvolari enjoyed racing the 1938 Auto Union at Donington. Today the world's biggest collection of single-seater racing cars is sited there

John Cobb's 24-litre Napier-Railton,
perpetual Brooklands lap record holder
at over 144mph, on the high banking,
in 1937. Cobb was killed attempting the
World's Water Speed Record on Loch
Ness post-war

When the 750Kg Formula roared its last, the 5.6-litre Mercedes
and 6-litre Auto Unions of 1937 were the most powerful Grand Prix
cars ever seen, just kissing 200mph in a straight line and wheel-
spinning their way out of slow corners with well over 550hp on tap.

In 1938 the AIACR brought a new Formula into operation,
restricting the capacity of supercharged cars to 3-litres and allowing a concession to unsupercharged cars of an extra litre and a
half—$4\frac{1}{2}$-litres 'unblown'. In addition a new *minimum* weight limit
of 850Kg was imposed, so with engine capacity halved and weight
up by at least 100Kg speeds were bound to tumble.

But so expert were the German engineers that race and lap
speeds tumbled much less than might have been expected. Both
Mercedes and Auto Union adopted V12-cylinder engines and
the racing seasons of 1938–39 saw 16 top-class motor races, of
which 11 fell to Mercedes-Benz, four to Auto Union and just one
—the Pau GP which began 3-litre racing in 1938—to the unblown
$4\frac{1}{2}$-litre French Delahaye of Rene Dreyfus. The 'name' drivers
were changing, Rosemeyer had been killed, and Nuvolari had
taken his place as Auto Union's star pilot. The Chemnitz team
had lost the services of Achille Varzi, who had become tragically
addicted to cocaine, while Dick Seaman won the 1938 German GP
for Mercedes, and lost his life when he crashed into a tree while
leading the 1939 Belgian event in the rain. Ex-racing mechanic
Herrmann Lang was the Mercedes star of the 3-litre Formula,
while Caracciola's rain skills stood him in good stead.

Both Alfa Romeo and Maserati produced eight-cylinder 3-litre
engines for the new class but they couldn't compete with the
Germans for sheer power, nor reliability. France virtually abandoned Formula racing, and the Italians concentrated more and

more on their 1500cc Voiturette racing, in which new Alfettas and Maseratis ruled supreme with no Germans around to upset the Pizza cart. Unfortunately for them, Mercedes built a pair of 1500cc cars—virtually scale models of the Grand Prix bolides—specially for the money-rich Tripoli GP, and they finished first and second!

Even so, Mussolini's machines ruled Voiturette racing immediately pre-war, and these designs were to have a profound effect when racing returned to a slowly recovering Europe after six years of bloody war had pulped the German racing departments at Stuttgart and Chemnitz.

In America neutralism saw racing continue into 1941, while Italy also kept on racing in Europe into 1940. While Maserati's 3-litre cars had had but one moment of real glory—when Paul Pietsch led the opening stages of the 1939 German GP—they rang the changes at Indianapolis. George Boyle bought a car for Wilbur Shaw, and he won both the 1939 and 1940 500-milers, and was leading the 1941 event when a wheel collapsed and he crashed heavily.

The effect of the European Maserati on the Indy establishment was similar to that of the Murphy Duesenberg on GP racing in 1921, and of the Miller single-seaters in the closing years of that decade. But now GP racing had forged ahead, and American constructors began modelling their cars on Maserati 8CTF lines, giving birth to the roadster designs which prevailed throughout the 'fifties. But one engine dominated Indy entirely, apart from the Maserati wins, and that was the 4-cylinder Offenhauser, which came into being in 1931 and which itself owed much to GP Peugeot practice!

Racing Renaissance

France had seen the birth of motor racing, its rebirth after the first world-wide conflict, and in 1945 it saw another immediate renaissance. September 1945 saw a celebratory race in Paris' Bois de Boulogne, honouring that city's liberation. Many pre-war racing cars were brought out of retirement, and the main event of the day was won by Jean-Pierre Wimille—a rising star of the pre-war years—in the single-seater Bugatti.

Immediately post-war racing was on a free-for-all basis due to the conditions in Europe, but the reformed and newly-titled governing body, the *Federation Internationale de l'Automobile* formulated new regulations for the years 1948–1953 (FIA).

Through their executive body, the *Commission Sportive Internationale* (CSI), they announced two Formulae. Formula A, the premier class, was for supercharged cars of up to 1500cc (pre-war Alfetta and Maserati Voiturettes, d'you see!), and for unsupercharged cars of up to $4\frac{1}{2}$-litres (like the pre-war Talbots and Delahayes). Formula B, which was intended as a less expensive training ground for new drivers, catered for 2-litre unblown or 500cc supercharged engines.

Before these regulations came into force, 1947 saw the revival of free formula racing at *Grande Epreuve* (generic term for top-class established Grand Prix) level. Alfa Romeo were the dominant team, with their supercharged 1500cc straight-eight engined Tipo 158 cars. Wimille, Varzi (cured of his addiction), Count Carlo Felice Trossi and works tester Consalvo Sanesi drove the cars, recording 1-2-3 wins in the Swiss, Belgian and Italian GPs.

Into 1948 and the imposition of the new regulations, Maserati produced a new tubular-chassised version of their pre-war blown four-cylinder designs, and notched a string of wins in the absence of Alfa Romeo, who won the Swiss, French, Italian and Monza GPs. At Turin the Italian GP saw the emergence of a new marque which was to have a profound effect on future racing. Enzo Ferrari was building sports and single-seater cars in his own right, and during the season his Formula A cars won at Garda, and Formula Bs at Bari and Florence.

Bugatti was out of racing, ruined by the war, but in their place Amédée Gordini's little Simca-based Voiturettes and Tony Lago's big Talbots kept France's blue colours in the winning circle.

Following their show of invincibility during 1948 Alfa Romeo withdrew from racing for 1949, leaving Ferrari and Maserati to contest the *Grandes Epreuves*. Raymond Mays and Peter Berthon, who between them had been responsible for the pre-war ERA Voiturettes, began the British Racing Motors project to produce a true challenger for the red cars, and work began at Bourne in Lincolnshire on an incredibly complex V16-cylinder centrifugally-supercharged car, with sponsorship and many components provided by British industry. It was to evolve into a completely over-bureacratized muddle. Frenchman Louis Rosier won for Talbot in the Belgian GP, running non-stop in his economical 'four-and-a-half', while Alberto Ascari—son of Alfa Romeo's star driver of the 'twenties—won regularly for Ferrari, as did Luigi Villoresi in Formula B.

The First World Champion
Then came the development which really put Grand Prix racing before the public on a glamorous level. The World Championship for drivers and constructors was inaugurated for the 1950 season.

Alfa Romeo returned to the fray, and with a further developed version of the now classic Alfetta Dr Giuseppe 'Nino' Farina became the sport's first World Champion. He won three of the six qualifying GPs—British, Belgian, French, Monaco, Swiss and Italian—and team-mate Juan Manuel Fangio took the other three; Farina taking the title on points with a better minor placing record.

The premier Formula was now known as Formula 1, the 2-litre unblown division becoming Formula 2 while a British-inspired class catering for tiny mainly rear-engined machines powered by 500cc motor-cycle engines, took the Formula 3 classification.

The first World Champion, Giuseppe
Farina, has his Alfa Romeo all crossed-
up at Silverstone, as the tail slides out
and he piles on corrective steering
lock

Ferrari progressed enormously in 1951, dropping their own
brand of blown 1500cc engine, and going the unsupercharged way
with $4\frac{1}{2}$-litre V12s. In the Championship races, which now included
revived German and Spanish GPs, Alfa Romeo won four rounds
to Ferrari's three. Alfa Romeo were at the limit of their development of the pre-war design, and they were beaten for the very first
time at Silverstone, where Fangio's compatriot Jose Froilan
Gonzales threw his big Ferrari round in a lurid manner, beating
Fangio's Alfa into second place and leaving grass and gravel all
over the roadway!

Fangio was the driver of the year, he took his first World
Championship title. But the year was fraught with problems, for
the BRM was not raceworthy, Alfa Romeo announced their now
over-stressed cars' withdrawal, and this left just Ferrari to face
Britain's never-never car, the long obsolete 1500cc Maseratis and
the lumbering old Talbots.

Race organizers were alarmed at the prospect of Ferrari-only
Grandes Epreuves for 1952, and so they abandoned Formula 1
in favour of the better-supported Formula 2 with its comparatively
inexpensive unblown 2-litre engines. The field included four-
cylinder Ferraris, six-cylinder Maseratis, French Gordinis, and
HWM, Cooper and Alta cars from Britain; as yet virtual also-rans,
but founding what was to become a great tradition. Italian domination could not be shaken, and Ferrari were unassailable.

Alberto Ascari won almost everything in sight in both 1952 and
1953—the two years of Formula 2 Championship racing—in which
he pocketed the proceeds of 11 title round wins, and took a double
World Championship.

The BRM V16 had been developed to race-winning form, but by the time its pitifully slow development had reached that point the Formula to which it had been designed was long dead, and it could only appear in Formula Libre events in Britain and New Zealand. Fangio and Gonzales were both drivers of the V16, as was a young recruit from 500cc Formula 3 racing whose name was Stirling Moss. . . .

Formula 1 came back into Grand Prix racing in 1954, when a new set of regulations came into force, limiting the use of super-chargers to 750cc engines, and allowing $2\frac{1}{2}$-litres unblown.

Mercedes return

The revived Formula 1 World Championship commenced in the Argentine in January, and Fangio won before his home crowd in a Maserati, beating the Ferraris of Farina and Gonzales. Back in Europe he repeated his win in the Belgian GP, and then came the advent of the much-heralded new Mercedes-Benz for the French GP at Reims, where Fangio relinquished his temporary leader-ship of the Bolognese team and took over a Mercedes cockpit in the footsteps of former Champions like Caracciola and Lang. He won first time out and ruled supreme until Gonzales and his young English team-mate Mike Hawthorn won for Ferrari in the British and Spanish GPs.

During 1955 the story was much the same, with Moss joining Fangio, the German Kling and Hans Herrmann in the regular Mercedes team, while Piero Taruffi also ran for them. Moss won the British GP to team orders, with the other three Mercedes following him across the line to fill the first four places. The German team's closest competition came from the new Italian Lancias, crewed by Ascari and his friend and mentor Luigi Villo-resi, plus dashing newcomer Eugenio Castellotti.

First time out in the 1954 Spanish GP the Ascari Lancia had stolen pole position on the starting grid, and in early-season 1955 races the cars proved their pace although they were rather tricky to handle. In the Monaco GP Ascari led the Mercedes roundly, but misjudged the chicane and crashed into the harbour waters. He was rescued wet and shaken, but within a week met a tragic death at Monza, unofficially practising in Villoresi's sports Ferrari. Lancia were in financial difficulties at this time, and late in the year Gianni Lancia closed-down his racing shop, and made a gift of all his competition material to Ferrari.

The year was riven and shattered by tragedy. First Ascari's death and then the dreadful Le Mans disaster in which the French-man Pierre Levegh crashed his Mercedes in an unavoidable col-lision before the main grandstand, and hurtling wreckage killed over 80 spectators and injured many more, marred the season. The French, Swiss, Spanish and German GPs were immediately cancelled and motor racing is prohibited to this day in Switzerland.

Britain had its own tragedy this year, when three drivers died
in the jubilee Tourist Trophy at the Dundrod road circuit in Ulster,
and America mourned Bill Vukovich, killed while on his way to a
third consecutive victory in the Indianapolis '500'—an event which
had become increasingly isolated and stagnant since the war.
Then, right at the close of the season, with Mercedes announcing
their withdrawal since they had achieved what they had set out
to do, and Fangio nursing his third World Championship, Britain
won a GP! The small Connaught concern had picked up a string
of minor placings in Formula 2 races in 1952–53 and had continued
with reliable performances in the new Formula 1. Then with the
amateur Tony Brooks at the wheel they beat a phalanx of works
Maseratis in the Mercedes-less Syracuse GP, emulating Sir Henry
Segrave's memorable San Sebastian victory of so many years
before.

The British challenge
Britain's stranglehold on 500cc Formula 3 racing had bred
drivers such as Stirling Moss and Peter Collins, and in 1956 the
former drove for Maserati and the latter joined his great friend
Mike Hawthorn at Ferrari. British drivers at last had the right
equipment to challenge the best that Italy, France and the Argentine could offer, and while Moss won the Monaco and Italian GPs,
Collins won the Belgian and French and Fangio the Argentine,
British and German. Peter Collins was set to take the World title
in his Lancia-engined Ferrari at Monza, but seeing Fangio aban-
doning in the pits he pulled in voluntarily and gave the elder man
his car, allowing the now legendary Argentinian to clinch his
fourth Championship.

In 1957 a new 1500cc Formula 2 was introduced, and Cooper
built an up-rated rear-engined car for the class based on their
Formula 3 and small-capacity sports car knowledge. They used
a four-cylinder engine produced by Coventry-Climax, which was
developed from an original design for a featherweight fire pump
for civil defence purposes in wartime. Coventry-Climax engines
appeared in many small-capacity sports racing cars in the early-
'fifties, Cooper and Lotus among them. Both marques—still
Climax-powered, were to have a profound impact on Grand Prix
racing and design.

Fangio won his fifth and last World Championship, for Maserati,
in 1957, but British industrialist Tony Vandervell, whose company
produced world-famous Thinwall bearings, had been developing
a green car since 1954 to beat the Italians. Known first as the Vanwall Special, and then as the Vanwall, the car used a four-cylinder
engine based partially on motor-cycle practice, and with a light
and very rigid chassis designed by Colin Chapman—the Lotus
constructor—and a super-streamlined bodyshell by Chapman's
associate, Frank Costin.

Vanwall for victory

Stirling Moss and Tony Brooks shared a Vanwall to win the British Grand Prix at Liverpool's Aintree circuit, beating the Ferraris of Luigi Musso and Mike Hawthorn.

Moss won the Pescara GP—in the Championship for the only time—for Vanwall, and the Italian GP warmed Vandervell's heart as three Vanwalls monopolized the front row of the starting grid, with all those 'bloody red cars' humbled behind. Moss won again.

One other event of note during the season was the Caen GP, a French non-Championship event, which Jean Behra won in the four-cylinder BRM, to mark the team's first major Formula 1 success after so many years of stumbling misfortune.

For Britain 1958 was a glorious but tragic season, as Mike Hawthorn won the World Championship in his Ferrari, with Moss runner-up for Vanwall and Tony Brooks third for the same team. Fangio turned out for his last race, the French GP at Reims, and finished fourth.

The old order was changing fast. Castellotti had crashed fatally while testing a Ferrari the previous year, and when Luigi Musso (who was intensely patriotic) overdid things in his Ferrari chasing Hawthorn at Reims, Italy lost her last top-flight racing driver. Mike Hawthorn's own joy in his World title was nullified by the stunning loss of Peter Collins, a few yards ahead of him at the Nurburgring in the German GP. Collins had won the British GP at Silverstone two weeks earlier . . .

But the Constructor's Championship was not to be forgotten, and for the first time the title was split between driver and car; Vanwall winning the Constructor's cup despite Hawthorn's fine personal title. Hawthorn retired at the end of the season, only to be killed in a road accident in January 1959. Uprated Climax engines in Cooper chassis began to appear on the Grand Prix scene, and Moss actually won the Argentine GP and the Frenchman Maurice Trintignant the Monaco race in Rob Walker's privately-owned 1.9-litre car. What it lacked in power it more than made up in easy handling and a tremendous power-to-weight ratio, for it was very light.

The 'kit car' championship

In 1959 Cooper obtained some full 2½-litre engines from Climax, and Australian Jack Brabham won them the World Championship. He won outright at Monaco and Aintree, while youthful New Zealand team-mate Bruce McLaren won the first Formula 1 United States Grand Prix on Florida's Sebring airfield circuit. Jo Bonnier, the bearded Swede, gave BRM their first-ever *Grande Epreuve* victory after 11 years' endeavour in the Dutch GP, while Tony Brooks won the French and German GPs for Ferrari.

For 1960, the last year of the very successful 2½-litre Formula, Jack Brabham had a string of wins in his Cooper-Climax, and put the final nails in the coffin of the front-engined Grand Prix car. But Moss won two races in a new rear-engined Lotus, and Colin Chapman's approach to racing design was much more scientific than the Cooper father and son team, who were intensely practical 'special builders' of the first order. They started the current theme of Formula 1 'kit cars'; building chassis to carry proprietary engines and transmissions, in marked contrast to Ferrari, Maserati, BRM and Vanwall who built virtually everything themselves.

Maserati had foundered financially after the 1957 season, Ferrari were struggling in the front-engined doldrums, and the British rear-engined cars just had Formula 1 in their pocket. But amid much dissension, the CSI changed the premier Formula for 1961–65, stipulating engines of only 1500cc in chassis heavier than most late-model 2½-litre cars, at 992lbs. In other words Formula 1 virtually disappeared and Formula 2 took over its title, while a new schoolroom class began for 1100cc cars, fostered in Italy in search of new drivers and known as Formula Junior.

Predominantly Fiat-engined Italian cars had dominated the Junior class in its first seasons, but once it became Internationally recognized in 1960–61 Lotus headed many British manufacturers into FJ production and swept the board, using Ford-based engines modified by the Cosworth Engineering Company.

But British manufacturers were happy with 2½-litre racing, and kicked against the FIA's decision to reduce capacity and impose hefty minimum weight limits. A crazily isolationist decision was

taken to continue racing the older cars in the so-called Inter
Continental Formula (up to 3-litres limit) and while Britons fussed
Ferrari went quietly ahead with a rear-engined F2-based design
and gained a huge advantage before British manufacturers got
the message and began to build 'proper' $1\frac{1}{2}$-litre F1 engines.

So the 1961 season saw a Ferrari walkover, again clouded by
tragedy. The Championship lay between Phil Hill and Wolfgang
von Trips, Ferrari team-mates, until in the deciding Italian GP at
Monza Trips collided with Scotsman Jim Clark's Lotus-Climax
and crashed fatally into the crowd. The American Hill became the
first of his nationality to win the World Championship, but it was a
cheerless title for him. Only the virtuoso performances of Stirling
Moss in an out-dated Lotus-Climax beat the Ferraris on sheer skill
at the series' two trickiest tracks, Monaco, and Nurburgring.

Towards the end of the season new V8 engines appeared from
Coventry-Climax and BRM, and 1962 saw the World Championship fought out between new stars; Graham Hill and Jimmy Clark.
Hill won the Championship in the last race—in South Africa—
when a bolt dropped out of Clark's Lotus-Climax's engine. Only
Ferrari and Porsche (from Germany) faced the horde of British
cars, and the only non-British win of the year was Dan Gurney's
first place for Porsche in the French event at Rouen.

'Kit cars', using proprietary engines were the order of the day
in 1963, after Porsche had withdrawn to leave just Ferrari and
BRM building every major part of their F1 cars, including chassis,
engine and gearbox. It was a Lotus-Climax year, Jim Clark winning a record seven *Grandes Epreuves* to take the title.

The story was to have been similar in 1964, but English ex-motorcyclist John Surtees put new life into Ferrari and stole the title in the last round at Mexico City, where Clark's Lotus ran out of oil and blew-up when leading, on the very last lap of the series! Graham Hill had been within striking distance of the title and it was the closest competition yet run for the World title.

In 1965 it was another Clark year, he won six GPs and clinched his second World title and secured the Constructors' Cup once again for Lotus and the Coventry-Climax engine concern. One fast rising star in the year's Formula 1 racing was a young Scot named Jackie Stewart, who had his first GP outing for BRM in January, and who won the Italian GP that September.

The return of power
For 1966 a new 3-litre Formula had been announced, doubling the engine capacity of the $1\frac{1}{2}$-litre 'noddy cars', which had nevertheless proved themselves the fastest GP devices of all time around a circuit. Chassis design had advanced enormously during the class' five-season life, and new, more scientific tyres made a major contribution to the increase in lap speeds.

The new Formula was well received, but Coventry-Climax had made their point by winning 54 per cent of all Championship races they entered from 1958–65, taking four World Championship titles for their customers and totalling 40 GP wins—24 in Lotus chassis, 14 in Coopers and two in Jack Brabham's own cars, built and raced under his own name since 1962. Now the company announced they would not be producing engines for the new Formula.

Just when Jackie Stewart and Jochen Rindt thought they had GP racing sewn-up, Jacky Ickx showed them how by winning the 1969 German and Canadian GPs. Here at Nurburgring the Belgian's Brabham leads the Scots World Champion's Matra

Colin Chapman of Lotus arranged a deal with Ford of Britain whereby they sponsored Cosworth Engineering to the tune of £100,000 to build a V8 F1 engine and a suitable four-cylinder unit for the new 1600cc F2 to start in 1967. These units would not be ready until the new year, and Climax supplied Lotus with bored-out 2-litre V8s based on the obsolete '1½' for the '66 season. Chapman hedged his bets by ordering new H16-cylinder BRM engines, but they were to be a long time coming.

BRM ran 2.1-litre versions of their 1965 cars until their complex new H16 should become raceworthy. This was based on the successful 1½-litre V8, with the cylinder banks laid flat, and what amounted to another 1½-litre 'flat' engine laid above them. The units crankshafts were geared together, and so one should have had a 16-cylinder 3-litre racing engine of enormous potential. The whole boiling was so complex and so unrealistic in conception it never recognized that potential.

Cooper found V12 engines from Maserati in Italy; Ferrari built their own V12s (of course); Brabham received a production-based V8 from Repco in Australia and Dan Gurney established his own Anglo-American Eagle concern to race at both Indianapolis and in Formula 1. More of Indy anon, but meantime an Eagle V12 engine was built by the Weslake company in England.

This was the line-up and in truth the season should have seen Ferrari winning all the way. But in mid-year Surtees had a dispute with the team and left, finding a seat in the Cooper-Maserati team, and with the proper 3-litre engines proving unreliable, and the stop-gap overbored 1½-litre engines just too impotent to be truly competitive, Jack Brabham won four GPs in a row with his Olds-

mobile production-based Repco V8, and simple workmanlike chassis frame. He was the first man to win a *Grande Epreuve* in a car carrying his own name ('66 French GP at Reims) and of course the first constructor to win the Drivers' Championship.

BRM's H16 engine was nursed across the line to win the US GP at the Watkins Glen circuit, but it was in the back of Jimmy Clark's Lotus at the time, and then in the final race at Mexico City John Surtees—a good development driver—brought the Cooper-Maserati onto song and scored the marque's first win since 1962. Cooper had started the new trend in GP racing back in 1958–59, but more scientific constructors had now stolen all their glory.

For 1967 the new Cosworth-Ford engine was late appearing, but when it did in the back of the works Lotuses the writing was clearly on the wall. Clark won four GPs, including the first-ever outing for the new cars at Holland's Zandvoort circuit, but it wasn't enough to combat the reliable Repco engines which took Jack Brabham to second place in the World Championship, behind his rugged New Zealand team-mate Denny Hulme who won the title in the final round at Mexico City.

Fords call the tune

It was clearly going to be another Clark and Lotus year in 1968, but after walking away with the South African GP he lost his life in an insignificant Formula 2 race at Hockenheimring in Germany, and this one tragedy virtually laid the Championship wide open. The Cosworth-Ford engines were now available for sale to other teams, and Stewart was driving a French Matra for entrant Ken Tyrrell—who had fostered Stewart's International career in its

early days—who used the V8 units, as did McLaren Racing, founded by Bruce McLaren who will be remembered as Jack Brabham's Cooper team-mate in 1959–61. Bruce had 'done a Jack' and was to win his first GP for his own marque that year.

But it was Graham Hill and Lotus-Ford who took the title despite their tragic loss, and again it was a cliff-hanger until Mexico City, where Stewart's Matra-Ford and Hulme's McLaren-Ford both hit trouble and lost their chance of the Championship. For 1969 the government-sponsored French Matra concern provided chassis for Tyrrell and Stewart, and he won six GPs in the season, equalling Clark's 1965 tally but falling short of the other Scot's seven-in-a-year record. Stewart took his first World title in superb style, fighting off challenges from the Ford-powered Lotus of Austrian Jochen Rindt and the Brabham of the youthful Belgian Jacky Ickx.

Rindt was Stewart's closest and most consistent competitor, of that there could be no doubt, and with a radical new Lotus for the 1970 season Jochen amassed a huge Championship lead only to crash fatally while practising for Monza. This was a dreadful blow to Lotus and despite a late-season Ferrari resurgence with an all-new flat-12 engined car driven by Ickx, nobody surpassed his points total, and so we had our first posthumous World Champion.

What had happened to Stewart? Matra had determined to run their own V12 engine for 1970, but neither Stewart nor Tyrrell could see a future in anything other than a Cosworth-Ford engine. Consequently they severed their ties with the predominantly aerospace and missile-manufacturing concern, and bought chassis from the newly-founded March concern in England. The Marches were hastily designed and built, and although they won three of the season's first four F1 races they had but one slightly freakish GP win when Stewart took the Spanish event. As the season progressed the March became less and less competitive, but with typically Tyrrell thoroughness a back-up had been commissioned and new Tyrrell cars were on the way.

The original Tyrrell-Ford appeared late in 1970 and came close to winning the US GP, and during 1971 Stewart's Tyrrell was near unbeatable, winning another six Championship rounds to clinch his second Championship, and entrant Tyrrell's first Manufacturers' Cup. Lotus went through a decline during the season, and for the first year since 1959 failed to win a single Formula 1 event. But they had a number of increasingly good finishes from their Brazilian team-leader Emerson Fittipaldi (who had won the 1970 US GP to ensure Jochen's late title) and he was to be the man of '72, winning the World Championship in an exemplary manner which is too recent to need recounting. This was Lotus' fifth World title in ten seasons' racing, and for the Cosworth-Ford engine it was the fifth title in a row! More than 50 Championship GPs had its only major opposition had come from Ferrari's flat-12.

The other classes
But meanwhile, what had happened to the minor Formulae, and in America? Formula Junior was Lotus and later Brabham dominated, all using Ford engines, until its demise at the close of 1963, whereupon it was replaced by two new single-seater classes; reviving the titles Formula 2 and Formula 3. Both were for 1000cc engines in lightweight single-seater chassis, but strict production-based limitations applied to F3 which were absent in F2, allowing a much higher performance from the latter.

Once again Ford engines dominated overall, but the first season of F3 racing in 1964 saw works-backed Coopers with BMC engines dominating everything in sight. After 1965 Ford engines dominated F3 racing until its modification in 1971, to cater for 1600cc production-based units with limited modification.

The small 1-litre Formula 2 was the preserve of Cosworth engines until 1966 when Jack Brabham had a complete monopoly using Japanese Honda units. A new Formula 2 came into being in 1967, when 1600cc engines using production blocks were specified, and again it was Cosworth-Ford all the way, the engine being virtually one-half of the Formula 1 V8. Ferrari also produced an engine for this class and had a brief moment of dominance, as did the German BMW company towards the end of the class' life in 1970. Current 2-litre Formula 2 racing came into being in 1972, using highly-modified production engines, while the most basic schooling Formulae in recent years had been the manufacturer-sponsored off-shoot divisions, like Formula Ford—using standard road-going Cortina saloon engines—and Formula Vee—which was born in America using standard Volkswagen Beetle parts.

Indianapolis went its own happy way until 1961, when Brabham took a Grand Prix-style Cooper-Climax there and finished ninth. Chapman built a special 4.2-litre Ford-powered Lotus for the 1963 '500' at American driver Dan Gurney's instigation, and Jimmy Clark finished second, blowing-off all the traditional Indy roadsters except one. Indianapolis racing introduced all kinds of items—like disc brakes, crash bars and driver safety harnesses—into standard use, but it was such a specialized and circumscribed form of racing that the advent of GP style lightweight, independently suspended rear-engined cars signalled as big a revolution as had occurred in Formula 1 in 1958–60.

By 1965, when Clark and Lotus-Ford won the '500' at their third appearance, the roadster or 'Dinosaur' as it became aptly known, was virtually extinct. Lap speeds soared around the rectangular $2\frac{1}{2}$-mile 'Brickyard', and then the age old Offenhauser engine was revived by the use of exhaust-driven supercharging, or 'Turbocharging' and the four-cylinder engine rapidly replaced the V8 Ford units as Indy's dominant power plant. Aerodynamics have played an exceptionally important part in Indy and American oval-track racing in recent years, particularly following the shat-

Times have changed: The 1968
Indianapolis 500-Miles very nearly fell
to the turbine-powered Lotus 56
'wedges', which combined four-wheel
drive with striking aerodynamics. Right:
The exhaust-driven turbo-supercharger
has made the age-old Offenhauser
engine the modern master at Indy.
Bottom: Wings grew too big in 1969 and
were banned. This one is on Denny
Hulme's McLaren

tering performances of the wedge-shaped four-wheel drive Lotus turbine powered cars—which never quite managed to win the race—and the blown Offy-powered McLarens—which did.

Aerodynamics played a similar part in Grand Prix racing in 1968–69 when strutted aerofoil devices were used to increase the traction and cornering powers of the cars without adding materially to their weight. Early in 1969 some of the constructors stepped too far into these largely unexplored realms and some bad accidents resulted in a ban on such devices, although they are still widely employed in modified and more cautious form, and have contributed vitally to ever-increasing lap speeds. Modern tyre technology has perhaps contributed more than any other single science to the rising speeds of modern-day racing, and even historic racing cars, driven by enthusiastic but hardly talented clubmen, have beaten the times of Fangio and Ascari and Nuvolari, purely because they are using modern tyre compounds and the tyre companies really do benefit technically from motor racing.

The use of such 'trickery' means that the modern Formula car is very far removed from anything which could be used on the road, and no longer does the plea that motor racing 'improves the breed' hold much water. What function it does fulfill today is largely one of publicity. Ford's £100,000 investment in a Grand Prix engine must be one of the most fantastically successful deals in commercial history, for to the public at large another Ford win in GP racing means much.

Top-class motor racing is still a forcing ground for ideas and a great spectator sport going its own way quite healthily and happily, owning little to its origins, and attracting stronger public interest and support than ever before.

2 RACING AND RACE SPECTATING

Motor racing is one of the world's fastest growing sports. In recent years Britain has probably had more racing events than any other country, although the United States is catching up fast with similarly multi-levelled meetings every weekend of the year.

All big International race meetings are run to similar schedules, with perhaps two and maybe three days of practice arranged prior to the day of the big race itself. Some events are a law unto themselves, like the Indianapolis 500-Miles, in which a complex (and to European eyes largely illogical) qualifying system runs throughout the previous month.

Before the race
If you have the time to spare, it's well worth going along to a race circuit for the practice sessions on, say, Friday and Saturday, in addition to the race itself on the Sunday. Movement is generally much less restricted on the practice days, crowds are smaller and you can usually gain cheaper access to the circuit itself, and to the paddock where the cars are prepared and maintained, and where public rub shoulders with press, mechanics, organizers, team personnel and drivers.

On a practice day you can get a much better 'feel' for the sporting spectacle about to take place. Seeing the cars stripped apart in their paddock bays will give an understanding of how they look, how they operate and how they compare to your own road car. You will have the chance to recognize the drivers at close quarters, and so put a face to the anonymous person lying in that car as it flashes past on the track, lost within his flame-proof overalls and all-enveloping helmet.

Most big races are supported by a programme of minor events. The British Grand Prix, for example, will have a supporting programme of races for single-seaters and modified saloon cars. Each race will have its corresponding practice sessions on the preceding days, with most time naturally being allotted to the Formula 1 cars in preparation for the World Championship.

During the practice sessions the drivers will be attempting to do two things; one, to adjust their vehicle to suit the circuit and so produce its optimum performance there—and two, to get the utmost out of that vehicle once the optimum adjustment has been achieved. The aim is a good starting position on the grid line-up. Every lap each car covers in practice is timed by the organizing club's timekeepers. At the end of each session a list of the fastest times for each car is published, and the fastest overall is awarded 'pole position', which is usually the inside position on the front row of the starting line-up, dependent upon which way the first corner goes. If it's a right-hander the pole is usually on the right-hand side of the track, and so on.

Alongside the pole position car and driver will be the next fastest in the practice list, and the third fastest will probably be placed on the extreme outside of the front row. Fourth fastest will be on the inside of the second row, with his car lined-up between the two inside cars ahead of him, and fifth fastest will complete the second row to his left. The third row will contain three cars, the next two and so on, leaving all the cars room to manouevre should the one ahead fail to leave the start-line cleanly.

This so-called 3-2-3 grid arrangement is fairly common, but other layouts are often used, such as 2-2-2 with two cars in each row, but alternately staggered to give them room for evasive tactics, or 3-3-3 as at Indianapolis, with the cars directly behind one another in what should theoretically be three parallel lines.

On the grid
Until recently all Grand Prix, and most other road races made what was known as a clutch start from their grids. In this the cars assembled in the order of practice times; with three minutes to go engines were started (by onboard self-starter since 1961, before which push starts and external starter motors were permitted), and at the fall of the starter's flag the whole field dropped their clutches and made a wild wheel-spinning charge off the line.

If any poor driver found his engine failing to start, gears failing to engage or his clutch failing to operate on the grid then he just had to sit there and pray, waving his hands in the air to warn those behind him of his predicament. As the flag fell cars would explode in all directions trying to avoid the obstacle, and in the rubber smoke from spinning tyres, and perhaps exhaust smoke from tortured engines, some hair-raising start-line collisions occurred.

Setting up a racing car

Opposite: Practice days are when everybody gets a closer look at the cars. Ferrari Chief Mechanic Giulio Borsari seems to have lost his workmate

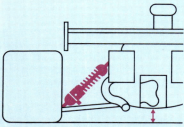 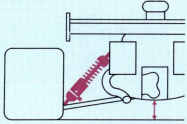

A racing car's ride height is important, and it is adjusted in one way by altering the lengths of the springs. This is achieved by screwing the bottom spring support up or down along the body of the damper fitted inside the spring

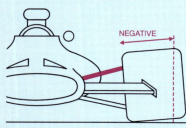 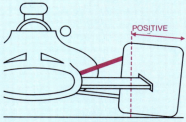

Camber is a problem for modern racing car designers. This is the amount of 'lean' a wheel has, and with modern ultra-wide tyres any camber up-edges the tread and gives a drastic reduction in grip. So adjustments to the suspension are made to remove major tendencies towards camber change as the suspension rises and falls

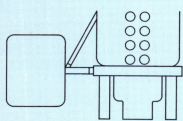 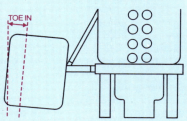

Toe-in is the angle of the wheels when viewed in plan; like a person being pigeon-toed. Extra toe-in on a car makes it steer and run accurately, but in racing cars it applies to the rear as well where it can aid traction and grip. Only very tiny amounts of toe-in are permissible

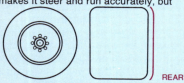 

Racing tyres make all the difference today between a car being competitive and being a back-marker. 17-inch wide rear tyres are not uncommon and narrower 13–14-inch covers are common on the front wheels. Wheel balance is critical and safety bolts hold the tyre to the rim to prevent it falling off should it deflate at speed. Pressures can be as low as 15lbs per square inch

Consequently in 1963 the US GP organizers introduced a system subsequently adopted for all GPs, in which the engines were started on a dummy grid, 100-yards or more behind the starting grid. With 30 seconds to go the whole grid would be signalled forward onto the grid proper, where they would pause momentarily on their marks before the flag fell and then made an otherwise normal clutch start. In this way most of the cars which were going to be reluctant starters were left behind on the dummy grid, out of harm's way.

A law unto itself

Now, at Indianapolis a very different system of qualification and starting is used. The race is always on Memorial Day at the end of May, and the whole month of May is given up to test and development runs and two qualifying weekends. Only on the first of these two weekends can one win the pole position, and only a four-lap flying stint counts towards that qualification. Each team informs the timekeepers of its intention to run a qualifying attempt with a car/driver combination, and if the driver is happy that his car is working at its optimum performance then he can signal to the timekeepers by waving a hand in the air, and his four-lap qualification stint begins next time round the $2\frac{1}{2}$-mile Speed-way.

Each lap is timed, and the average speed of the whole quartet qualifies for the grid position. As the day goes on so faster four lap speeds can 'bump' a driver/car combination further down the grid, but at the end of that first weekend nobody else can attack the front row positions.

The second weekend therefore sees those who were 'bumped' or who failed to get a clear four-lap run on the first weekend attempting to qualify again, and irrespective of how fast they go they cannot tackle the all-important pole position. So you have the peculiar situation of having potentially extremely fast cars buried well back in the starting grid, and this can be dangerous

Three pictures, three kinds of start. Below: The Le Mans-type start of the RAC TT at Ards in 1933. Right: The rolling start behind a pace car at Indianapolis in 1966. Bottom: The grid start of the 1968 Italian GP at Monza (note the 3-2-3 grid)

on a circuit as confined and narrow as Indianapolis has become for today's 199mph lap speeds. The start is made by running the grid of 33 cars (11 rows of three cars each) round on a number of pace laps behind a course car, slowly building up speed until the starter is happy that the cars are holding station well in their correct positions and then the pace car will pull off into the pit-lane (hopefully without crashing at the end of it as happened in 1971!) and the race is on, the front row accelerating into the first turn with the whole field boiling on its tail. Mishandled rolling starts have caused a fatal accident in 1958, and an enormous multiple crash occurred right on the start-line in 1966.

This type of rolling start allowed Indy car designers to dispense with low gears in the days of the roadsters during the 'fifties, but when Colin Chapman and Lotus appeared there in 1963 they re-introduced a road-racing type low gear to allow high-speed re-entry to the race following pit stops for fuel and tyres. In fact Indy is such a specialized circuit that two-speed gearboxes have been common; low for leaving the pits and high for the race, while brakes are barely used except on entry to the pits and many of the old roadsters could only turn left!

Road-racing is much more demanding in many ways, and dependent upon the punch available from the engines four-to-five speed gearboxes are common. Rolling starts are becoming more widely used in road-racing, today, particularly in World Championship sports car events where the fields are often very large, and in Canadian–American Challenge Cup (Can Am) style, unlimited capacity sports car racing, in which big sports cars can use the leeway afforded by being already under way when the flag drops!

One of the most exciting start methods was the Le Mans-type start. Here, all the cars would be lined-up in echelon against the pit counters, while their drivers would line-up opposite them across the track. At flag-fall the drivers had to sprint across to their cars, leap in, start-up and slide away into the race. This was used, as the name suggests, for the Le Mans 24-Hours, and stemmed from the earliest days when crews had to erect their car's hoods before starting the race! In recent years, with the advent of full safety harnesses to retain the drivers in an accident, the Le Mans start has fallen from favour. It was a difficult choice for drivers to make, whether to make a fast start and struggle to don their harnesses once under way, or to lose time at the start and play safe by fastening the harness before joining the race. There were some nasty accidents in the opening laps and consequently these exciting starts are now banned. This is a shame for there used to be some hilarious stories of muffled Le Mans starts, with gearlevers disappearing up trouser legs, and feet catching in steering wheels.

But whatever type of start is used the actual programme on race day—at least for a road race—will be similar. For the first

supporting race the field will take to the track for a warming-up or reconnaissance lap.

In this lap the drivers will be warming their engines, transmissions and tyres. Warming tyres today is crucial, for specialized racing compounds only work satisfactorily at a certain temperature. If they run cold they do not generate the kind of grip the driver might expect, and if they run too hot they may suffer damage and break-up. You will often see drivers sawing at their steering wheels on these laps, or making great smoking, wheel-spinning getaways from the pits, and what they are desperately trying to do is to gain the greatest advantage from their tyres, and to make them hot and sticky.

Types of tyres

While talking about tyres, today sees different covers being used dependent on the weather conditions. In dry weather an almost completely bald, slick tyre will be used, which places the maximum amount of rubber on the road and so gives maximum cornering, acceleration and braking power. In wet weather water would gather beneath these tyres like a wedge, force its way between the tread and the road surface and the car would slither madly out of control. This is known as aquaplaning.

So different tread compounds and tread designs are used for very wet weather. The rubber itself (although today actual organic rubber is replaced by synthetic compounds) will be much softer and will work at its best in the lower temperatures to be encountered. A wet-weather tread pattern is deeply grooved with numerous drains and gutters which will duct away gallons of water every second, to prevent that fatal watery wedge.

Using these wet weather tyres in the dry would be as fatal as using dries in wet conditions. The tyre tread is unstable if it exceeds a certain temperature, and in the dry it will rapidly heat-up and just jellify or fall to pieces—a dangerous condition known as 'chunking'. Therefore a third type of tyre has been developed for use in changeable weather. Known as an intermediate, which combines the best features of wet and dry tyres with a compound which can operate over a reasonably wide range, whether it is being roasted by sudden sun, or drenched by showery rain. The heavier a car is then the greater work its tyres have to do, and so these bigger vehicles usually have the added handicap of having

51

to use a harder, less grippy tyre, which can absorb a higher
running temperature. Thus the heavier a car is then the greater
its performance penalty becomes, because in extreme cases
(such as a single-seater compared to a saloon car) the less-grippy
tyres it must use.

At the end of their warming-up lap the drivers will have a good
idea of how their cars handle on full fuel tanks, their machines
will be ready to race and they will have a good idea of how the
circuit has changed since their last lap round it. Oil might have
been laid down which will make certain corners slippery, and so
on. The start will be given in the ways I have described and then
the drivers have that awesome dive into the first corner.

Following the race

To follow the course of the race, lap chart blanks are provided in
most race programmes. As each car passes your vantage point,
the system is to jot down their numbers in the order on the chart,
so that after each lap you have the race order represented by the
column of numbers in your programme.

As the race progresses the fast leaders may well catch and
overtake the tail-enders, in other words they will have lapped
them and will be running one whole lap ahead of them. This will
mean that the back-marker will come round for several laps perhaps between the second- and third-place cars on the road, but
his number must not be recorded in that position, for then you will
find you have jumped the last lap, represented by the previous
column. The back-marker's number must always go to the foot of
the appropriate lap column behind that on which the leaders are
running, and if you keep your chart correctly this will just occur
naturally as you note the cars' passing on every lap.

Keeping a lap chart can be difficult, particularly on a short
circuit with many cars flashing by in tight groups, but it is a challenge and it gives you a deep understanding of the course of
events. Often you get a better idea of what is happening then the
commentators can provide over the public address system.

I have several times lap charted entire 1,000Km sports car
races, which becomes incredibly complicated as scheduled and
unscheduled pit-stops take place, and which really isn't worth the
trouble! In shorter club-type races it's a good idea, particularly
for the novice race-goer. As the race progresses lap times should
fall as heavy fuel loads are burned off. There comes one point
during any race at which each individual car reaches its optimum
performance for that circuit, on that day. As more fuel is burned
and the car becomes lighter, it may start to perform less well, and
of course a thousand things can fail which make it slower and
sicker. In this way a driver may make a late attack on the leaders,
or the leaders themselves may just increase speed and charge
away into the middle distance as the race progresses.

Lap chart

Race	Lap Record	Race Distance
German GP	7mins 20.1secs 116.07mph	14 laps 198.64 miles
Date July 30 1972	**Lap Distance** 14.19 miles	**Starting Time** 14.30
Circuit Nurburgring	**No. of Laps** 14	**Weather** Warm, dry

No	Driver/Car	Laps 1	2	3	4	5	6	7	8	9	10	11	12	13	14
4	Ickx/Ferrari	4	4	4	4	4	4	4	4	4	4	4	4	4	4
1	Stewart/Tyrrell	10	10	10	10	2	2	2	2	2	2	9	9	9	9
2	Fittipaldi/Lotus	9	2	2	2	10	10	10	10	9	9	1	1	1	10
10	Peterson/March	2	9	9	9	9	9	9	9	1	1	10	10	10	17
7	Cevert/Tyrrell	1	1	1	1	1	1	1	1	10	10	6	6	(6)	5
12	Reutemann/Brabham	12	12	12	12	12	12	20	20	20	20	17	17	17	11
9	Regazzoni/Ferrari	20	20	20	20	20	20	6	6	6	6	5	5	5	26
8	Amon/Matra	7	7	7	7	14	14	14	14	17	17	11	11	11	28
20	Pescarolo/March	21	21	14	14	7	6	17	17	5	5	26	26	26	6
3	Hulme/McLaren	15	15	15	6	6	7	7	3	11	11	(19)	28	28	7
21	Pace/March	6	6	6	15	15	15	15	(7)	19	19	28	7	7	
15	Schenken/Surtees	22	14	22	22	17	17	3	5	26	26	7	(19)	19	
6	Beltoise/BRM	14	22	3	17	22	3	5	16	(16)	28	16	16	16	
22	Stommelen/March	3	3	17	3	3	5	16	19	28	7	15	15	15	
11	Hill/Brabham	17	17	18	5	5	16	19	11	15	16	8	8	8	
14	Hailwood/Surtees	19	18	(21)	19	16	19	11	26	7	(15)	21			
18	Wisell/BRM	18	19	19	16	19	11	26	28	8	8				
17	Ganley/BRM	26	5	5	(23)	11	26	28	(15)	21	21				
5	Redman/McLaren	5	23	23	11	26	28	8	8						
16	De Adamich/Surtees	23	26	16	26	25	(25)	21	21						
26	Fittipaldi (w)/Brabham	11	11	26	25	28	(22)								
19	Merzaris/Ferrari	16	16	11	28	(21)	8								
25	Walker/Lotus	28	29	29	21	8	21								
23	Lauda/March	29	28	28	27										
27	Bell/Tecno	25	25	25	(29)										
29	Charlton/Lotus	(27)	27	27	8										
28	Beuttler/March	8	8	8											

■ Black Flag　　(29) Pit Stop　　— 1 lap behind　　= 2 laps behind

Above: Emerson Fittipaldi's 1972
World Championship-winning 'John
Player Special'; the now classic Lotus
72. Below: The blood-red of Italy;
Jacky Ickx's Ferrari 312B2

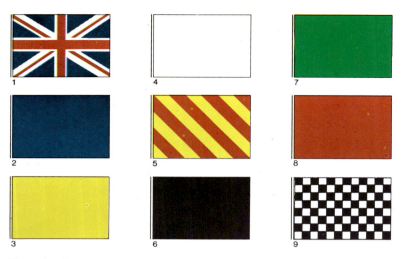

Race tactics

Race tactics are so many and varied it is impossible to describe them. I have seen Grands Prix where the first two cars run nose to tail for much of the distance, and it appears to be a complete stalemate between the two. But what has been happening is that the trailing driver has been tailing the leader to test his potential, watching for possible openings, and then with just a few laps to go he will blast past when that opening appears and just storm away to win. On the other hand great excitement is caused when a car trailing by 20 seconds is seen to be gaining by a second a lap, with twenty laps to run. But whether it is gaining due to extra effort or because the leading car is slowing, or being slowed by traffic, can only be resolved by observation. Watching out for all these things can make race spectating more interesting, and as you gain knowledge it can become totally absorbing.

The marshals

All race circuits are marshalled by numerous officials appointed —usually with no reward other than an outlet for enthusiasm—by the organizing club. Some of these marshals control traffic arrangements and run the programme from the paddock. Others are stationed to control the crowd—at least in Britain while most Continental circuits recruit police for this purpose!

The flag marshals have the most essential job of all. Their internationally-recognized flags and their meaning are shown here and as will be seen they are all meant to warn and inform. Quick reactions and the ability to make the *right* decisions are vital for good flag-marshalling, and it can often mean the difference between safe racing and some very serious damage and injury. Probably the best flag marshals in the world are those of the British Racing & Sports Car Club, who regularly received highest praise from the sports car circus for sustained accuracy during the life of the BOAC race at Brands Hatch. Best rescue crews in the world are almost certainly those based at the American super-Speedways, like Indianapolis where fire tenders and wrecker trucks actually *meet* crashing cars.

Flag signals: The national flag (1) starts the race. The blue flag (2) held steady means you are being followed, and if waved shows that somebody is passing you. The yellow (3) means caution held steady, and great danger if waved, while the white (4) shows that ambulances or service vehicles are on the course. The striped flag (5) warns of oil and the black (6) shown with a car number orders a pit-stop. The green (7) shows that a former hazard has now been removed, and the red (8) means 'all cars stop immediately'. The chequer (9) signals the finish of the race, waving at the winner and being held steady for those who come behind

Below: On the climb to Nurburgring's Karusell turn, the 1972 German GP field show how to straight-line an ess

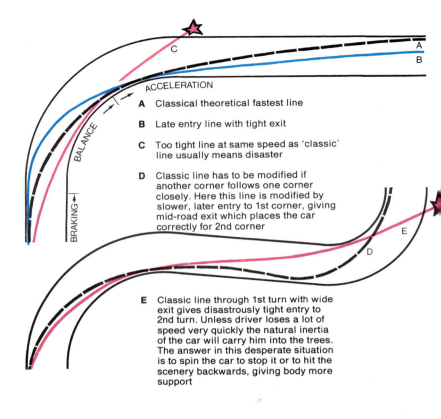

ACCELERATION

A Classical theoretical fastest line

B Late entry line with tight exit

C Too tight line at same speed as 'classic' line usually means disaster

D Classic line has to be modified if another corner follows one corner closely. Here this line is modified by slower, later entry to 1st corner, giving mid-road exit which places the car correctly for 2nd corner

BALANCE

BRAKING→

E Classic line through 1st turn with wide exit gives disastrously tight entry to 2nd turn. Unless driver loses a lot of speed very quickly the natural inertia of the car will carry him into the trees. The answer in this desperate situation is to spin the car to stop it or to hit the scenery backwards, giving body more support

F Classic line modified for ess bends

G Classic line for first turn puts driver wrong for second part, more wrong for third, and so on until he either loses a lot of time or runs out of road at the fifth part of the ess. There would be virtually no changes to overtake in this section, for the driver would then be bound to arrive at one of the component corners too fast and on the wrong line

Try running a pointer along these lines at a constant speed and you will realize why the man who gets part one wrong and yet presses on gets into real trouble in the later part of the ess

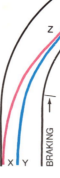

Z

↑

BRAKING

X Y

A situation often seen in racing where the 'classic' line theoretical driver (X) comes up against an experienced 'racer'. If Driver X takes his classic wide entry to this turn then the challenging Driver Y has a wide open space to occupy on the inside. He dives into it on a tight line, stealing X's piece of road at point Z, forcing X wide and making him lose speed if he intends to stay on the road. Y can only get round if he slows more than he would on a normal solo line through the corner, but he has forced X to slow more and has gone ahead. This is why a battle for 2nd and 3rd place in a race will often fall away from the leader, because the drivers are slowing each other down, and also why race lap speeds are usually slower than those in practice where cars are running against the clock rather than against one another

Below: The special challenge of the 2.5 mile banked Indy circuit is such that the brakes are hardly used, the car slowing on engine over-run with the throttle closed. There is no speedometer in modern racing cars, the drivers judging their speed by the engine revolutions per minute (rpm) shown on a 'rev counter' instrument. Since this test run, eight years ago, improved aerodynamics and tyres have allowed higher gearing to give greater speed and better grip through the turns, raising the lap record to 199mph *average*, with 220mph on the straightaways and 180mph-plus actually through the turns

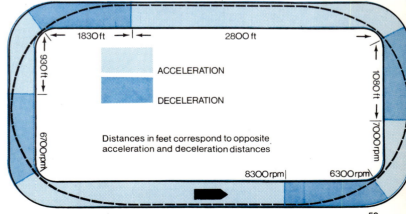

1830 ft   2800 ft

930 ft

1080 ft

6700 rpm   7000 rpm

ACCELERATION

DECELERATION

Distances in feet correspond to opposite acceleration and deceleration distances

8300 rpm   6300 rpm

Top: Jackie Stewart's ELF Petroleum-
backed Tyrrell-Ford 005. Far right: The
Marlboro-BRM's are colourful. Right:
Brand-new for '73 was this Yardley-
McLaren M23

3 THE RACING CAR

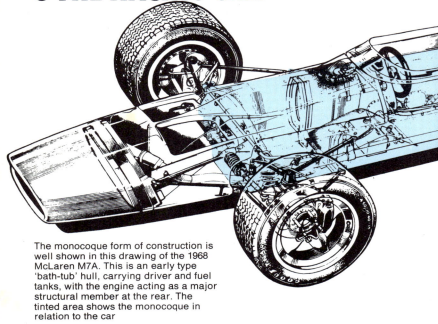

The monocoque form of construction is well shown in this drawing of the 1968 McLaren M7A. This is an early type 'bath-tub' hull, carrying driver and fuel tanks, with the engine acting as a major structural member at the rear. The tinted area shows the monocoque in relation to the car

The modern racing car, whether it is a Grand Prix single-seater, one of the off-shoot manufacturers' formulae kiddy cars or a giant sports-racer, is very far removed from the road cars we see and use every day.

In fact competition cars have differed from production models in many respects since the earliest years of the century, but with modern 17-inch wide tyres and the suspension systems necessary to contain them, regulation safety chassis design and aerodynamic aids to road-holding the two types are now further divorced than ever before.

The monocoque
All modern leading Formula single-seaters are now built on some form of 'monocoque' principle. In other words their structural stiffness—which is very important to their cornering and straight-line stability—derives from a so-called 'single-shell' chassis. This type of construction was used on the famous Indianapolis Cornelian of 1915, and in sports cars like the Jaguar D-Type and E-Type, until 1962 when Colin Chapman of Lotus introduced the form to Grand Prix racing.

The strength of his Lotus 25 derived from what looked like a bath-tub of folded aluminium sheet. This consisted of enclosed box sections on either side which contained the rubber bag fuel tanks, with bulkheads binding these boxes together at front and rear. The driver sat in the 'tub' between the tanks, with the engine and rear suspension attached behind his shoulders and the front

Illustration by Bill Bennett

suspension just ahead of his toes. The open top of the tub was enclosed by a streamlined glass fibre nose cowling, and the whole thing was lighter and stiffer than the then universal tubular spaceframe chassis.

The modern monocoque is little changed in basics, although more sophisticated shapes and materials have been adopted. Most modern single-seater monocoques are shaped to house their massive fuel tanks well within the wheelbase, around the car's centre point, for this makes the complete vehicle much more swervable and easy to drive. In recent years this concentration of weight has extended to moving the water radiators which cool the engine from their conventional nose mounting to a hip mounting on either side of the monocoque in line with the driver's shoulders.

This feature has allowed perfectly wedge-shaped chisel noses to be adopted, their flat upper surfaces acting as a huge 'dive plane', the action of the airstream on them forcing the car down onto the road surface, and aiding traction. What downthrust is applied by the nose of the car must be balanced up by some kind of aerofoil at the rear, for if the car runs badly nose-down at speed its rear wheels will become light and the car will be unstable. So rear aerofoils are used which are strictly limited in width and height to prevent them growing to the dangerous heights adopted in 1968–69. Trailing edge tabs on these aerofoils and twin horizontal fins on either side of the nose section give fine adjustment which can 'trim out' the car to achieve a perfect balance.

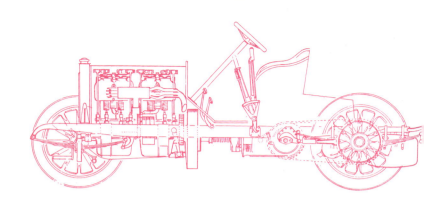

Racing design, from ancient to 'nearly modern'. From above, 1903, 1908 and 1914 Mercedes, while the large cutaway shows the 6-litre 520hp Auto Union 16-cylinder of 1936

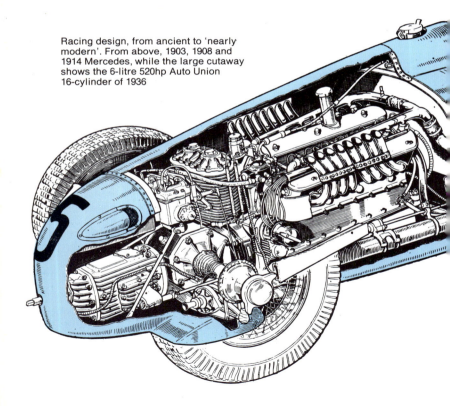

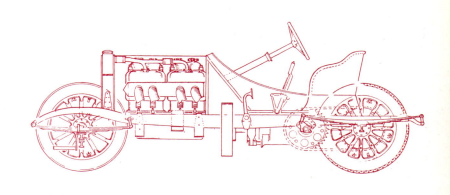

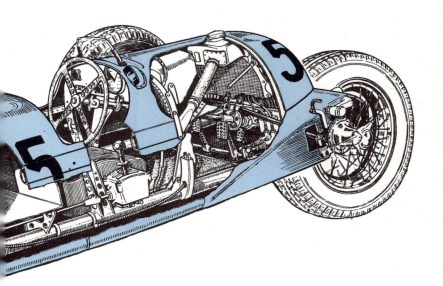

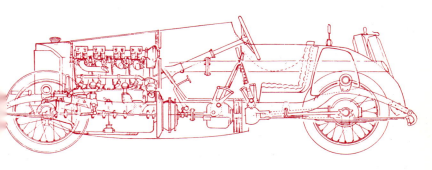

Sicily's Targa Florio. Nino Vaccarella
from Palermo is waved on his winning
way in the 1971 event, his Alfa Romeo
T33 leading a Lancia

Internal monocoque structures vary widely, Ferrari for example using a composite type in which a load-bearing tubular frame is reinforced by sheet metal riveted and bonded into place as 'fixed bodywork'. Chassis for the Cosworth-Ford Formula 1 engine terminate immediately behind the cockpit, and the engine itself is sufficiently strong to carry the gearbox and rear suspension. Just four bolts attach the engine to the back of the monocoque hull, and the other components are in turn bolted-up to the engine.

Ferrari use a horizontally-opposed 12-cylinder engine of their own design which is much flatter than the rather tall Cosworth V8 and this allows them to build low cars with a very low centre of gravity, which is advantageous to their cornering power. This engine is hung under a high-level rearward extension of the monocoque hull, and the whole assembly is extremely neat.

Modern sports-racing cars in the main use monocoque hulls, built along similar principles to the single-seaters, but with two-seater width cockpits between the fuel-tank-carrying sponsons. Front suspension is usually carried directly into the monocoque's front bulkhead around the driver's foot pedals, while at the rear it is normal for the engines to be mounted in a tubular steel frame which mates up to the monocoque's rear cockpit bulkhead. Often this frame just acts as a kind of steadying structure, while the cylinder block of the engine is stressed and acts as a major structural member, feeding cornering, braking and acceleration loads from the suspension into the main body of the car.

The whole thing is clothed in all-enveloping bodywork which is closely governed by the regulations in size and in the equipment it carries. Once again aerodynamic downthrust and balance are vital to the car's performance around a circuit, and indeed with the enveloping sports car body it is much more critical than on a single-seater, where the bodywork may not extend beyond the mid-point of the wheels front and rear. Small strips, fins and tabs often appear riveted or taped on a sports car's body, and these are always added in search of that aerodynamic balance so vital to the modern car's stability and handling at speed.

The spaceframe

The CanAm-winning Porsches of 1972 were unusual for today in being spaceframe cars; that is being based on a frame of welded lightweight tubes, in this case made of space-age magnesium alloy. This structure was exceedingly expensive, yet very light and rigid, which is the object of all designers.

Regulations insisting that fuel tanks be sheathed in metal really brought about the monocoque monopoly in top-class single-seater racing, but they can be stiffer than a spaceframe of comparable weight. Arguments against them are that they are much more difficult to repair after suffering crash damage (try repairing a crushed beer can!). A spaceframe can be easily heated and

straightened, or if badly damaged the bent tubes can be simply cut away and replaced by new. Monocoques do tend to absorb impacts more efficiently by their tendency to crush, and many drivers have had remarkable escapes from injury in which the monocoque chassis' outer skin has been destroyed but the inner-skins, alongside the driver's body, have remained true.

Safety requirements are all-important in modern regulations, and crushable structures alongside the load-bearing part of the car's chassis are now recommended to minimize the chances of a fuel tank rupture or driver injury, and in the event of fire an onboard fire extinguisher system can be fired off which fills the cockpit and engine bay with foam. Full seat harnesses are now almost universal, consisting of shoulder straps to retain the upper half of the body, a lap strap to retain the torso and crotch straps which prevent the recumbent driver 'submarining' down into the nose of the car in a head-on impact.

Left: The spaceframe chassis is just a maze of tubes carrying engine, fuel tanks and suspension, as seen in this 1961 Championship-winning Ferrari V6.

Below: Progress brought the 'deformable structure' protected monocoques of 1973 like John Surtees' new TS14 seen here

Other features

Most racing gearboxes do not have synchromesh as do most road cars, and yet they engage speedily and efficiently with a type of engagement system which is not designed to last 50,000 miles, and which is often in bad shape after 250 miles but which is just strong enough to do this specialized job. Brakes are enormous compared with those used in road cars, for as much time can be saved by shortening the period necessary to slow the car down as can be saved by reaching shattering speeds along the straight. Exit speed from one corner will determine the maximum speed along the straight before the next corner, and so everything must be going for the car and its driver if he is to produce a competitive lap time. Disc brakes are used which are hollow with air ductings built-in to dissipate the enormous heat build-up caused by a 1300lb car slowing from 200–100mph in less than 400 feet. Minor Formulae cars, like Formula 2, 3, Ford, Vee and so on, are built to more economic prices than Formula 1 or Indy cars, and many of the basic schoolroom classes, like Formulae Ford or the French Formule France and Formula Super Vee demand tubular space-frame chassis as an anti-inflationary measure.

So these are the machines which are carrying those drivers out there, and let's finally have a quick look at the regulations which govern them for 1973 (overleaf).

Formula 1 Engine capacity, not more than 3-litres unsupercharged or 1½-litres supercharged. Not more than 12-cylinders. Minimum weight (without ballast), 575Kg, 1258lbs. Regulations govern the size and design of the bodywork and wings, the chassis structure, fuel and oil systems and safety features such as roll-over bars and onboard fire extinguishers. Current Formula runs until December, 1975.

Formula 2 Engine capacity, not more than 2-litres, supercharging banned. Engines must be based on 1,000-off production units. Weights are fixed at 450Kg, 990lbs with a 4-cylinder engine; 475Kg, 1045lbs with a 6-cylinder and 500Kg, 1100lbs for more than 6-cylinders. Body and safety regs are similar to those for F1, and current Formula runs until 31 December, 1975.

Formula 3 Engine capacity, not more than 1600cc and not more than 4-cylinders, based on 5,000-off production units. A throttling flange severely restricts the flow of air into the engine, thus limiting its power output, and tyre tread widths are also limited to 8-inches. Minimum weight is only 440Kg, 968lbs. This Formula runs until 31 December, 1974.

USAC (Indianapolis) Regulations This 'formula' is very complex, attempting to equate supercharged and unsupercharged engines and production-based 'stock block' engines. Capacities are 2.65-litres blown, 4.5-litres unblown and 5.82-litres for pushrod 'stock-blocks'. Maximum car length is 15ft, maximum width 6ft 10ins, minimum wheelbase 8ft and minimum track 3ft 11ins. Minimum weights are 1500lbs supercharged and 1425lbs unsupercharged, and safety rules and wing limitations have to be observed.

There are many other Formulae and groups of regulations to which International races are run. The FIA Group 1 caters for absolutely standard saloon cars, Group 2 for modified saloons, Group 3 for series-production Grand Touring (GT) cars, Group 4 is for modified GTs and Group 5 is now a blanket World Championship-type sports car class with divisions at 2-litres and an overall 3-litre limit. Group 6 was for 3-litre prototype sports cars but is now defunct and Group 7 is for 'anything goes' two-seater sports racing cars such as are used in the famous CanAm Championship in Canada and America, and in European Interseries events.

Other single-seater Formulae, which generically come under the FIA's Group 8, include Formula 5000, for big single-seater cars powered by 5-litre production based engines, Formula Ford for spaceframe single-seaters using standard British Ford 1600cc engines, Formula Vee for 1300cc VW-based cars, Formula Super-Vee for 1600cc VW-engined cars with special chassis and suspensions, Formule Renault in France for 1600cc Renault Gordini engined machines and the new Formula Sudam for South American racing, using up to 2-litre production-based engines.

4 THE MEN

Racing drivers, just like men in any other profession, come in all shapes and sizes. Some are extrovert and gay and others more introverted and quiet, yet there are some definite traits which seem common to all the top-liners, both ancient and modern.

Makings of a driver
Like most sportsmen, or successful businessmen, the will to win and a deep-seated streak of determination seem inseparable from the top men. This doesn't exactly make them the most likeable, pleasant and friendly kind of characters, but some camouflage it better than others! Physically a particularly good pair of eyes seems essential. There have been successful racing drivers who wore spectacles, like Rudolf Hasse who won the 1937 Belgian GP, Masten Gregory who was a works Cooper driver and a regular Formula 1 dicer in the late 'fifties, and currently Andrea de Adamich, the Italian F1 pilot who has the European Touring Car Championship and World Championship sports car race wins to his credit. But none of these drivers was exactly star material; and never in the class of the greats like Caracciola, Nuvolari, Ascari, Fangio, Moss, Clark and Stewart. This particular septet were all gifted with exceedingly acute eyesight, enabling them to recognize and assess situations in an instant, giving excellently conditioned high-speed reflexes the chance to operate that vital split second before those of any 'mere mortal'.

A lot has been said and written about the enormously fast re-action times needed for race driving, but generally speaking I do not believe this holds true. In normal everyday situations the aces' reactions would probably be on a par with any normally fit being of similar age, but put them in a motor car and their conditioning to this particular environment, and the assessment and control of situations at high speed would be exceptional. While our normal

man in the street would be totally absorbed in controlling a car through a particular corner at 90mph, the aces would probably be capable of negotiating the same turn in the same car at 110mph or more, virtually subconsciously, with much of their mental capacity still going spare!

If you are driven around a circuit by one of the perennial also-rans of Grand Prix racing your reaction would probably be one of breathless wonderment. When you realize that these people stand nowhere on the proven scale of ability your estimation of the true aces knows no bounds. The point is that race driving is not a matter of jut-chinned, barrel-chested heroes striding to their cars, smashing the accelerator to the floor and hanging on like grim death, driving like lunatics with no regard for tomorrow.

Most of the aces of yesterday and today are married men with certain responsibilities. Most of them value their own necks and what risks they do take are carefully calculated and controlled.

Keeping things under control
But keeping a high-powered racing car under control is a matter of balance, of 'feel' for the car's behaviour and of anticipation for what it is going to do next. Drivers have their cars 'set-up' to handle in the way they like. Nearly all of them like a car to be stable and run true in a straight line. Nearly all like a car which brakes squarely and efficiently, but through the corners one finds vast differences in preference.

Some drivers like a car which loses adhesion first at the rear, and which can be thrown through a corner under power with the tail hanging out and the front wheels turned in the opposite direction to that of the corner, in what is known as an oversteering drift.

In its purest form a drifting car will have been induced to slide through a curve with all four wheels pointed straight ahead, the car arcing through the corner with the maximum possible amount of power feeding through to the road surface. A skilled and sensitive driver will have induced the slide on the entry to the corner, caught the tail by applying opposite lock on the steering, and then by balancing engine power (on the accelerator) against the steering lock he will maintain the slide through the curve.

Tazio Nuvolari is said to have perfected the art of drifting a car with Alfa Romeo during the 'thirties, while Juan Fangio gave an unforgettable display of the art in the 1957 French GP at Rouen. During the $1\frac{1}{2}$-litre Formula there just wasn't enough power available to overcome the road-holding of the chassis, and the cars flashed round corners quicker than their predecessors but looking dull in comparison as they cornered as though they were on rails. Once the 3-litre Formula reached full development certain cars recovered the ability to drift, and then tyre and aerodynamic developments became so sophisticated as to bring them back almost to the 'cornering on rails' stage.

The driver's position
This doesn't make the cars any easier to drive, although their controls and steering are much lighter today than in years gone by. The driver of today's cars lies almost on his back in a tailor-made fitting seat, within the close confines of his cockpit. A tiny steering wheel, a stubby little gearchange lever and a set of shaped foot pedals are his controls. Everything in these cars happens at high speed. The steering movements are tiny relative to the movement of the road wheels, the gearchanges are made by inch movements of the lever, modern fuel injected engines are sensitive to the slightest touch on the accelerator pedal, and the brakes are hard and extremely powerful. To save seconds into the corners the drivers use a 'heel-and-toe' technique to operate brakes, throttle and clutch all at the same time to change down into the turns, without coming off the brakes.

Suspension
The suspension of the modern racing car is highly developed and carefully designed to maintain firm contact between the rubber compounds of the tyres it carries and the road surface upon which the car is running. With modern wide-tread tyres the wheels have to remain vertical to the road surface at all times. They must no longer lean in or out on bump or droop (the two extremes of suspension movement) as they did in the early years of independent suspension when tyres were narrow and could compensate for such 'camber' changes.

If modern wide wheels and tyres take on camber, the tyres up-edge and instantly that vital contact patch between the tread and the road surface is slashed. If the wheel is under power it will spin wildly; if under braking it will lock, and either way the car will lose its knife-edge stability and attempt to spin across the road.

So the design and adjustment of the suspension is critical. Drivers can adjust their car's suspension to suit their driving requirements, so that they feel happy and at home with its cornering behaviour. Adjustments can make either the rear wheels lose adhesion first (the oversteering already discussed) or the front wheels, whereon the car will attempt to straighten-out the corners and run wide instead of faithfully following the arc traced by the front wheels.

These requirements can alter from circuit to circuit. If there are many hairpins the driver might require some oversteer, so that he can easily provoke a tail-slide by tramping on the power. An understeering car would run wide in this situation and could prove a considerable embarrassment!

On the other hand a fast circuit with many long curves would be anathema to a violent oversteerer, and the stability offered by a basic understeer would give the driver a secure feeling of stability much required at very high speeds.

In 1937 the great Mercedes and Auto Unions were reaching 195mph along the Masta Straight at Spa (at a point just after a left-right kink between houses in Masta hamlet!), and in 1966–67 with the extra wind-resistance from modern-sized tyres top speeds had actually fallen to 175–180mph. Yet lap speeds had risen enormously in the same period, not all of which increase could be attributed to circuit improvements.

The most comparable of all circuits was the 14.2-mile north circuit of the Nurburgring, which Bernd Rosemeyer lapped in 1937 in 9 mins 53.4 secs, or 85.62mph. This was with a 520bhp 6-litre Auto Union. In 1957 Fangio's fantastic German GP-winning drive left the lap record for the same circuit at 9 mins 17.4 secs or 91.53mph. His Maserati 250F was a 260bhp $2\frac{1}{2}$-litre. But progress continued, and in 1965 Jimmy Clark's Lotus-Climax lapped the 'Ring in 8 mins 24.1 secs, at 101.22mph, with a 210bhp $1\frac{1}{2}$-litre! Since then the circuit has been much modified, bumps eased, a slower chicane inserted but many other sections speeded-up and the 1972 record stands at 7 mins 13.6 secs, 117.81mph, but cannot properly be compared with earlier times.

Everything happens faster for today's driver, but this is not to criticize those who went before. Some people claim that it makes no difference what kind of car these people drive, the problems remain the same, but I cannot accept this argument.

What skill and courage must it have taken to hold a hurtling German car of the 'thirties at 190mph on a narrow and bumpy straight, knowing that 120mph had to be scrubbed off before one stood a chance of negotiating the bend that was fast approaching. Today's cars are smaller, snugger, more an extension of the driver's being. Circuits are wider, smoother and better marked. At 190mph on a comparable straight one could probably go beyond the 200 metre warning board before braking for the coming curve, which in a modern car one could negotiate with no problems at It is in the speed differential that the vital difference lies, and the way of comparing driver performances is the 'tenths' system of effort.

A driver driving at ten-tenths, or maximum effort, in 1937 would have been on a near suicidal knife-edge between triumph and tragedy at 70mph through our hypothetical curve. Today's driver at ten-tenths would be cornering at more than 110mph through the same turn. In both cases driving at nine-tenths would produce a lap time less than the optimum of which the car was capable, while an attempt at eleven-tenths driving would wind up in the trees or in the ditch in 1937, and in the Armco Motorway barrier or sleeper-faced bank in 1973.

This then is what the top-class racing driver faces and the kind of character which predominates is single-minded, determined and possessed of the physical abilities we have noted. Let's have a look at some of motor racing's modern greats. . . .

Jackie Stewart, World Champion Driver,
1969 and 1971. Right: Emerson
Fittipaldi, youngest-ever World
Champion, 1972

Jackie Stewart b. 11 June 1939
Every age has one driver who sets the pace in his time, and the
canny Scot from Dunbarton is today's standard-setter. He was the
younger son of the town's Jaguar dealer, and elder brother Jimmy
raced Jaguars and Aston Martins during the 'fifties. The younger
Stewart wanted to excel at something different, took up clay
pigeon shooting and reached Olympic standard before embarking
on a race-driving career.

He has a happy knack of excelling at almost anything he
attempts, and after successful first seasons in 1962–63 in British
club-racing he was signed-on by Cooper F3 team patron Ken
Tyrrell for 1964. He won every race entered except two, won in
Formula 2 before the end of the year and made his F1 debut in
South Africa's non-Championship Rand GP that December, driving a Lotus.

He signed for BRM in 1965, winning the Italian GP and placing
third in his first World Championship. He had a bad crash at Spa
in 1966 which set back his development, and BRM's engine problems kept him out of contention for 1966–67. In 1968 Tyrrell ran
Matra chassis with the new Cosworth-Ford V8 engines for Stewart,

Overleaf: Denny Hulme, World
Champion Driver, 1967; Jacky Ickx,
twice runner up and one of the fastest
of them all. Graham Hill, World
Champion Driver, 1962 and 1968, Indy
winner 1966, Le Mans 24-Hours winner
1972

and the new combination won three GPs and challenged for the Championship before hitting trouble in the last round.

In 1969 he won his first World Championship in the Tyrrell Matras, taking six qualifying GP titles, and then in 1970 Tyrrell's new Marches proved a failure and it took all-new Tyrrell-Fords to help Stewart to his second World title in three years in 1971, when he won another six GPs. In 1972 he was less lucky, winning only three more and losing his title to new Lotus number one Emerson Fittipaldi. Nevertheless, Stewart led more GPs for longer, during the season, than did his Brazilian challenger.

Stewart is a master of the media, and as accomplished a TV performer as he is politician and business man. He is one of the movers towards added safety in motor racing, and a lot of his demands seem to many devotees to exceed the realms of reality. Stewart's widespread popularity with the general public is not altogether shared by the sport's enthusiast following, and his restricted race programme doesn't help in this respect.

Nonetheless, nobody can possibly challenge his ability, and he is all set to break Jimmy Clark's great record of 25 Championship Grand Prix victories. Stewart is married (wife Helen) and lives at Begnins in Switzerland with two small sons, Mark and Paul.

Emerson Fittipaldi b. 12 December 1946
Younger son of a Brazilian motor racing journalist, Emerson had as rapid a rise to stardom as did drivers like Clark and Stewart before him. At 17 he began racing karts and in 1966 took to motor racing. He and elder brother Wilson set up a tuning and accessory business, well-publicized by their victories on the tracks, and in 1967 Emerson won the Brazilian Formula V Championship.

In May 1969 he arrived in Europe to race a Formula Ford, won three out of nine races and was instantly promoted to Formula 3 with a Lotus backed by the British Jim Russell Racing Drivers' School. He won the Lombank F3 Championship, and entered Formula 2 for 1970, also being signed by Lotus for the British GP. He finished eighth. In his next GP, the German, he was fourth. He crashed his new Lotus GP car in practice for the Italian GP, shortly before team leader Jochen Rindt lost his life, and then in fairy-tale style he won the US GP to put the Austrian's points total beyond reach and ensure his posthumous title.

During 1972 Emerson notched a string of good results but no wins in Formula 1, and then in 1972 a string of successes in the black-painted John Player Special Lotuses brought him a well-deserved World Championship. He drove in more F1 races than any other driver, and took no less than nine first places! His World Championship was brilliantly well merited, and this calm and pleasant young Brazilian could well become a second Fangio. He is married (Maria-Helena) and shares a house in Lausanne, Switzerland, with brother Wilson and his wife.

Denis Hulme b. 18 June 1936
'Denny the Bear', rugged son of a wartime New Zealand Victoria Cross-winner, first raced an MG TF in local hill-climbs in 1956. He bought himself a Cooper and won the 1960 'Driver to Europe' scholarship, two years after Bruce McLaren, and raced widely in Formula Junior.

Quiet and impassive, Denny became a Brabham mechanic, and never a man to try to sell himself he had a hard time making ends meet. In 1964 he became Jack Brabham's F2 team-mate and went from strength to strength, eventually winning a place in the F1 team during 1965. In 1966 he was capable of winning Grands Prix, and in 1967 he did so, winning at Monaco and Nurburgring to clinch the World Championship.

Denny freely admits that 'making speeches is the worst thing in the world' and he didn't really cash in on his title as other drivers have done. Late in his Championship season he joined the New Zealand McLaren team for north American CanAm Championship sports car racing, and this competition he and Bruce McLaren were to dominate for five seasons.

He was Rookie of the Year at Indianapolis in 1967 driving an Eagle and won the CanAm title in 1968 and 1970, despite suffering from burns suffered at Indy and from the stunning death of his friend Bruce in a testing crash.

During 1972 Denny shot back to prominence as a Formula 1 driver, and he won the South African GP in his Yardley-McLaren and was well in the running for the Championship, finally being ousted from second place by Stewart's late-season charge.

He still retains his tough exterior, but is now more comfortable in public. He is if anything much under-rated as a driver, but admits that he just hates to race when it's raining. . . . He built much of his own luxury house at Weybridge in Surrey, England, where he lives with wife Greeta and children Martin and Adele.

Jacky Ickx b. 1 January 1945
Another motoring journalist's son, Jacques Bernard Ickx is a Belgian. An often moody but on his day brilliantly fast driver, Ickx has twice been World Championship runner-up. He flashed to prominence in 1965 while doing his national service as a tank driving instructor! Another of Ken Tyrrell's protégés he shone as Stewart's number two in their 1967 Matra F2 team and won the

European Championship. He was snapped up by the Gulf Oil-backed JW Automotive long-distance sports car team and had great success with their Mirage and Ford GT cars including winning Le Mans by 200 yards in 1969.

Ickx made his F1 debut for Cooper in the 1967 Italian GP and with Ferrari in 1968 he won the French GP but crashed and broke a leg in Canada. In 1969 he raced Brabham-Fords, and won the German and Canadian GPs from Stewart and Rindt, who at that time seemed to think that Grand Prix racing was their game. In 1970 he returned to Ferrari winning three GPs, and in 1971 he added one more. During 1972 he led the Ferrari team, winning the German GP and several rounds of the World Sports Car Championship which the Italian team totally dominated, winning all events they entered.

Jacky Ickx is very much his own man. He resigned from the Grand Prix Drivers Association because he disagreed with the way they operated and has always been prepared to race almost anything anywhere. He is at his best as team leader, and in his Tyrrell days it was noticeable how his performances slumped when Stewart was around. It is only this lack of consistency which has separated him from racing's ultimate prize, for today's stars cannot afford temperament.

He is married to the daughter of a Belgian amateur driver and industrialist—Catherine—and lives just outside Brussels.

Graham Hill b. 15 February 1929

Now, at 44 the doyen of active Grand Prix drivers, Graham Hill fought a long hard fight to reach the top. He had his first race in 1954 when working as a mechanic just to be around motor racing. He found his way into the Lotus team, driving first sports cars and later their unsuccessful F1 machines, and then in 1960 transferred to BRM. He stayed with them until 1966, winning their first World Championship in 1962, and then accepted Ford money to join Lotus for 1967.

With the new Cosworth-Ford engines he and Jimmy Clark were dominant in F1 events, but they started too late to steal the Championship from Hulme and his Repco-Brabham. After Clark's death in early 1968 Graham took up the cudgels for Lotus and won the next two GPs in Spain and Monte Carlo, and rounded off the season by winning in Mexico to clinch his second World title.

In 1969 he was overshadowed by team-mate Rindt, and crashed very badly in the US GP, suffering severe leg injuries. But he was racing again in the South African GP beginning the 1970 season although a shadow of his former self, at the wheel of Rob Walker's private Lotus-Ford.

In 1971 and 1972 he had poor seasons with Brabham, save for a non-Championship F1 win at Silverstone and only rarely showing the type of determined consistent driving of his peak years. But he drove for Matra-Simca at Le Mans in '72, sharing with Henri Pescarolo, and won. He had won the Indianapolis 500 in 1966 driving a Lola-Ford through the carnage of the start-line accident, and thus became the first driver ever to have the World Championship, Indy and Le Mans victories to his credit—a unique triple crown.

Despite his flagging success Graham Hill remains one of the sport's best possible ambassadors with his outgoing personality and flashing wit. He is one of the few top-line drivers to maintain his home in England (most fleeing crushing taxation) and lives with wife Bette and children Brigitte, Damon and Samantha, in North London.

Mark Donohue b. 18 March 1937
Quiet and friendly Mark Donohue is rapidly replacing Andretti as America's 'wonder boy'. He is a unique combination driver-engineer, and graduated from Brown University in 1959 with a BSc degree in mechanical engineering. He started racing with a Corvette sports car that same year, and in 1961 won a National Championship road-racing with an Elva Courier. In 1965 he won two titles, with widely divergent Mustang saloon and Lotus 20 single-seater, gaining the Sports Car Club of America's Driver of the Year award.

Roger Penske provided Donohue with a Sunoco Special Lola for the 1966 CanAm Championship, in which he was second, and

in 1967 he won the US Road Racing title and was highest-placed
American in CanAm with a Penske McLaren. He repeated as
USRRC title holder in 1968 and added the Trans-American sedan
Championship for Chevrolet. He became the Martini & Rossi
Driver of the Year, and in 1969 was fastest rookie qualifier at
Indianapolis and finished seventh to win the Rookie of the Year
award. In 1970 he was second at Indy, led much of the '71 race
before retiring his Penske McLaren and then won the race in an
updated McLaren in '72.

Porsche of Germany chose the Penske-Donohue duo to run
their fearsome turbocharged CanAm sports car programme, and
Mark did much of the development work which produced such a
potent machine. Unfortunately he did not reap just reward, for he
crashed in a pre-race test at Atlanta and damaged his knee when
an insecure engine cover came adrift. George Follmer took over
the plum Porsche drive, and became the first non-McLaren driver
to take the Championship for six years!

Mark Donohue made a startling F1 debut in a McLaren in the
1971 Canadian GP, finishing third, and is due for Formula 1 racing
in the future. 'Captain Nice' as he is sometimes called, is married
(Sue), and lives in Newtown Square, Pa, with sons Michael and
David.

Mario Andretti b. 28 February 1940
America's greatest all-rounder of the 'sixties, Mario Andretti was
born in Italy and caught the racing bug while watching the Italian
GP of 1954. He raced Stanguellini FJ cars before emigrating to
the USA with his family at the age of 19.

In America he soon took up stock car racing, and then graduated
to the midget car circuits. In 1964 he began to drive big circuit
track cars under United States Auto Club auspices, in the Championship which includes the prestigious Indianapolis race. He
won the USAC National Championship in 1965, 1966 and 1969 and
was runner-up in 1967 and 1968. He was third in the Indy 500 first
time round in 1965, took the pole in '66 and '67 and finally won the
race for the STP team in 1969.

Lotus signed him on for selected F1 races in 1968–69, when
they did not clash with USAC commitments. He took pole in his
first race for them, the US GP, and drove three races for them in
1969. Sadly he was given the unsuccessful four-wheel drive car,
and then in 1970 STP bought him a March which he raced five
times, again without success. Then in 1971 he joined Ferrari—
whom he regarded as his 'home team'—and he won the South
African and Questor GPs for them, plus sharing several sports
car victories as he did again in 1972 although his Formula 1 season
was less impressive.

Andretti is married (Dee Ann) and has three children (Barbra
Dee, Michael and Jeffrey), and the family live in Nazareth, Pa.

Peter Revson b. 27 February 1939

Wealthy son of one of the founders of the Revlon Cosmetics concern, Peter Revson began motor racing while in college in Hawaii in 1960. He drove a Morgan sports car so vigorously he was asked not to come again! He spent some time being bored by an advertising executive job on Madison Avenue, still racing as an amateur, and then 1963 found him in Europe with an FJ Cooper.

In 1964 he financed his own F1 programme with an obsolete Lotus but made no impression and then returned to America save for some Formula 2 and 3 European events during 1965, highlight of which was a fine victory in the Monaco F3 event. In 1966 he drove a Ford GT40 in Championship sports car events, scoring class wins in three rounds and from 1967 he stayed in the USA, driving TransAm sedans and USRRC/CanAm sports cars.

The likeable but sometimes excitable American came back to prominence in 1969 when he qualified a Repco-Brabham in 33rd and last starting place at Indianapolis, and soared through the field to finish fifth. He later won a USAC road race in the Indy Raceway Park with the Brabham.

In 1970 after Denny Hulme burned himself in a testing incident, 'Revvie' was co-opted into the McLaren Indy team. In CanAm he drove a Lola and proved to be the McLaren team's major opposition. Consequently Gulf-McLaren team manager Teddy Mayer signed him on for both Indy and CanAm racing in 1971 and while the track racing saw him take Indy pole position and finish second he became the first American driver to win the CanAm Championship in a most lucrative season's racing.

For 1972 Revson joined the Yardley-McLaren F1 team and put up some fine performances to finish fifth in the World Championship. His return to European style racing proved him a driver of completely transformed stature, and as true top liner.

Peter Revson is a bachelor and lives in fashionable Redondo Beach, California, where he can indulge a passion for boats and fishing in the Pacific.